why boys are different

why boys are different

and how to bring out the best in them

Bonnie Macmillan, B.Ed., M.A., Ph.D.
Research Associate
Department of Psychology
University of Hull
United Kingdom

BARRON'S

Contents

First edition for the United States, Canada, and the Philippine Republic in 2004 published by Barron's Educational Series, Inc.

First published in Great Britain in 2004 by Hamlyn, a division of Octopus Publishing Group Limited, 2–4 Heron Quays, London E14 4JP, Great Britain

American edition Copyright © 2004 by Barron's Educational Series, Inc.

Copyright © 2004 by Octopus Publishing Group Limited

All inquiries should be addressed to:
Barron's Educational Series, Inc.
250 Wireless Boulevard
Hauppauge, New York 11788
http://www.barronseduc.com

International Standard Book Number 0-7641-2870-1
Library of Congress Catalog Card No. 2003114004

Printed in China
9 8 7 6 5 4 3 2 1

introduction

Maybe you're a new mother facing the challenge of bringing up a boy. Perhaps you're a father concerned about your son's progress at school. Boys are in the news these days, and the stories don't always make very happy reading. Truancy, reading failure, suicide, violence, hyperactivity, autism – whatever it might be, there appears to be more of it among boys.

But, how much truth resides in the popular portrayals of what it means to be male in the world today? Are boys really so very different from girls? Are they more vulnerable? How can parents make the best of any differences that do exist? How can differences be seen for what they really are, not deficiencies, but attributes that can be built upon? This book answers these questions and aims to help you raise a brighter, happier, healthier boy.

The brain is the key to sex differences

Of course, there are obvious anatomical and reproductive differences between girls and boys, but it is their brains that hold the real key to their differences. As early as seven weeks after conception, the release of hormones triggers a unique pattern of brain development in boys, resulting in a brain that is surprisingly different from that of a girl in its structure, its sequence of development and its way of operating.

In the last twenty years, new, non-invasive methods of investigating brain structure and function have been developed. Magnetic resonance imaging (MRI) and functional MRI (fMRI) utilize magnetic fields and radio waves to produce high-quality computerized images. An EEG (electroencephalogram) records electrical activity in the brain, and ultrasound imaging uses sound waves to produce computerized images. None of these procedures involves X-rays or injections of radioactive materials, so they have made it safe to investigate brain structure, development and activity in the young and even in the unborn. For the first time, scientists are beginning to be able to make direct links between brain structure and observed behavior. With the field virtually still in its infancy, new findings are being made, disputed, confirmed and elaborated every day. There are now concrete neuro-anatomical reasons that help to explain why boys are more competitive than girls, why they excel at visual-spatial skills and why boys are the more emotional sex. No one before has properly analyzed and provided adequate explanation for boys' underachievement in reading – this book is the first to detail the specific biological reasons why current methods of reading instruction (which are now becoming popular worldwide) are particularly bad for boys.

Are boys more influenced by their environment than girls?

If hormones are the first architect of the brain, then environmental experience is the second and is an equally important one. Recent neuroscience findings make it clear that almost everything a child experiences has a profound effect on how the brain grows and develops. Every cuddle, conversation, taste sensation and visual surprise causes actual physical changes in the young brain, changes that determine just exactly how it "wires" itself up.

This is where parents can make a tremendous difference. You can significantly enhance your child's intellectual and emotional potential – and not just during the early years. Although brain growth is at an all-time high during the first five years of life, new research has revealed that the male brain continues to grow and be affected by environmental experience well into adolescence and the late twenties.

Boys and girls will always be different

The brains of boys and girls differ at birth, each sex set to follow a different course of brain development. As a result, from birth boys and girls behave differently and tend to elicit different responses from those around them. In addition, society's gender stereotypes still contribute to shaping boys' and girls' behavior in different ways, affecting their language and their emotional, motor, intellectual and social development.

For genetic reasons, boys may be even more affected than girls by their physical and environmental experiences. When compared with girls, more boys fall at the opposite ends of any spectrum – that is, more boys are academically gifted or more suffer from stuttering, for example.

Unless we understand biological, brain-based sex differences, however, it is impossible to make informed assessments about which environmental factors might harm or benefit one sex more than the other. Brain research helps to explain, for instance, why secure parental connections throughout childhood and adolescence are especially critical for boys.

This book is different

Controversy surrounds the topic of sex differences. Traditional debate has nearly always danced around which sex is smarter, which is weaker and so on. However, with the advent of new findings from brain imaging studies, this book places the discussion of sex differences in the context of biological fact. Clearly, neither sex is better. They are simply different. As the neuropsychologist Diane Halpern points out, to ask which sex has the better brain is like asking which sex has the better private parts.

Although boys are probably more like girls than different from them, it is their differences that make them special. This book will tell you how to make the most of those differences so that you can bring out the very best in your boy.

1 brain development

1 What makes a boy different from a girl?

"Boys are different from girls, aren't they?" Ellen asks her husband on the drive home from visiting her sister and family. She smiles at two-year-old Sophie, fast asleep in her car seat. Earlier, they noticed how differently Sophie's cousin Christopher played and behaved (he's also two). Are *all* boys so different from girls? Are the differences a reflection of personality and upbringing? Or, do real differences actually exist between boys and girls? Ellen is expecting their second child – a boy – in a couple of months, so the answers to such questions suddenly seem to matter.

Biologically they are obviously different, but it is boys' brains that are the real key to the differences. Although *genes* play an early role in pre-programming the sex of the brain, we now know that it is the exposure to certain *hormones* early in life that is responsible for producing sex differences in the brain. Even in the womb, the fetus is exposed to different levels of male and female hormones, and throughout a child's life these influence brain structure and the way in which it operates. But genes and hormones are not the whole story. What happens in the *environment* also plays a part, shaping the brains of boys and girls differently.

Reasons boys' brains are different
○ *Genes* pre-program the brain to be male or female.
○ Male *hormones* influence brain structure and organization.

Did you know...?
A boy's large appetite starts early. Research shows that women who are pregnant with boys eat more than those carrying a girl. At birth, boy babies weigh on average 100 g (about 3½ oz) more than girls do. But how does the mother's brain receive the message to eat more? No one knows for sure, but the secretion of testosterone from the testes of the male fetus is the major suspect.

The beginning of a boy

12 midnight	Billions of sperm are swimming toward the egg
3 a.m.	A "male" sperm has swum as far as the uterus
7 a.m.	This sperm reaches and penetrates the egg; reactions in the egg stop entry of other sperm
10 a.m.	The nuclei of egg and sperm fuse
8 p.m.	First cell division occurs
4 days later	Embryo has divided five times to form a clump of 32 cells
From 4 days	"Baby" and placenta begin to develop
By 7 weeks	The embryo forms testes that release testosterone
At 8 weeks	Embryo officially becomes a male fetus
By 4 months	Male sexual organs are visible on ultrasound

○ Boys and girls interact differently with their *environment* (which includes other people), with their experiences shaping their brains differently.

Biological beginnings

How is a boy made? The genes, of course, are the first in on the act. There are two kinds of sperm: those carrying an X chromosome and those carrying a Y chromosome. An X-carrying sperm will program the egg it fertilizes to become female, whereas one with a Y chromosome will grow into a boy.

Sperm bearing a Y chromosome are known to swim faster but die quicker than their X-chromosome-bearing counterparts, which is why the timing of intercourse can favor one sex or the other. Making love just as an egg has been released from an ovary (signaled by a slight rise in body temperature) will raise the chances of a boy being conceived.

For the first few weeks, however, the embryo is of neutral sex – it is neither male nor female. Then, just seven weeks after fertilization, the presence of the Y chromosome triggers the release of two hormones: testosterone and MIS (mullerian inhibiting substance).

The first hormone, testosterone, sees to it that the development of male internal organs (the testes) gets under way. The second hormone prevents the embryo from developing into a female. Had it not been for the presence of the Y chromosome, and the two hormones released at this time, the embryo would have developed into a baby girl – nature's usual or "default" option.

While the hormones are responsible for making the fetus look male (with the growth of the male sexual organs), the same chemicals are also at work shaping the most important organ of all – his brain.

1 What do hormones do to the brain?

Hormones, mostly testosterone in males and estrogen in females, have powerful effects on the brain, often accelerating growth. Male and female hormones shape the brain differently, however, affecting how boys' and girls' brains will be structured, how they will operate, and the sequence in which they will develop.

As mentioned already, the Y chromosome pre-programs the release of male hormones about seven weeks after gestation. This increase in testosterone levels causes the male sex organs to form, and the newly formed testicles then churn out further substantial amounts of testosterone.

Testosterone levels rise three times in a boy's life – in the womb, shortly after birth and, finally, during puberty. Each time this happens, the way the brain grows and develops is altered permanently. Each time, the brain becomes more and more male. Although there is still a lot we don't know about the extent to which testosterone causes brain changes during these periods, with the advent of new monitoring and brain-scanning technology, something new is being discovered almost every day.

The effects of testosterone before birth

Only very recently have scientists discovered that the period from seven to sixteen weeks in the womb is literally life-changing for the tiny male fetus. During this period, testosterone levels rise, reaching a peak between twelve and sixteen weeks. This is a critical period during which any alterations to the correct amount of testosterone can permanently alter the

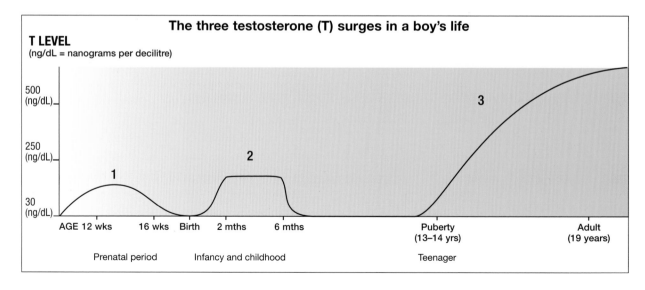

The three testosterone (T) surges in a boy's life

T LEVEL
(ng/dL = nanograms per decilitre)

500 (ng/dL)

250 (ng/dL)

30 (ng/dL)

1

2

3

AGE 12 wks   16 wks   Birth   2 mths   6 mths   Puberty (13–14 yrs)   Adult (19 years)

Prenatal period   Infancy and childhood   Teenager

Transforming testosterone

In addition to causing male sexual organs to form in the male fetus, testosterone

○ makes the brain slightly bigger in the speech perception region on the left side;

○ begins to organize the brain to operate in a more specialized way than the female brain;

○ makes the right hemisphere of the brain slightly larger than the left, unlike the more equal-sized hemispheres of girls;

○ structures the brain differently from females, enhancing certain spatial and perceptual abilities;

○ initiates a different sequence of brain development than that which occurs in girls' brains (speeding the development of some motor and spatial abilities while slightly slowing the development of other verbal and perceptual abilities).

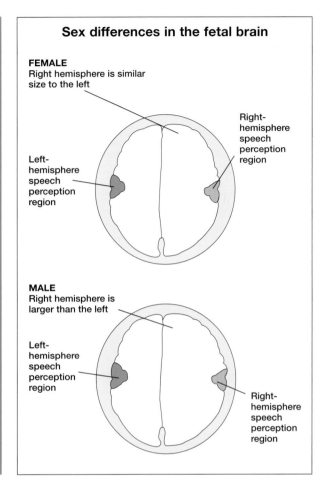

Sex differences in the fetal brain

FEMALE
Right hemisphere is similar size to the left

Right-hemisphere speech perception region

Left-hemisphere speech perception region

MALE
Right hemisphere is larger than the left

Left-hemisphere speech perception region

Right-hemisphere speech perception region

development of both a boy's sexual organs and his brain. Israeli scientists have found that regular ultrasound examinations, beginning a few weeks after this time, can distinguish a male from a female brain.

Testosterone alters a boy's brain before birth in
○ its structure,
○ its operating system,
○ its sequence of development.

Sex differences in brain structure

The brains of all mammals are divided into two halves, known as hemispheres. Scientists have discovered that, at just 29 weeks after gestation, a small region in the fetal brain is bigger on the left than in the corresponding region on the right. This area is involved in perceiving speech sounds, and when the electrical activity of fetuses' brains is measured at 30 weeks, the left sides of their brains respond more to these sounds. Here we have an early glimpse that the left hemisphere in both girls and boys is going to be designed to handle language tasks better than the right.

What is particularly interesting, however, is that the left-bigger-than-right asymmetry of this region is more pronounced in males – an early example of a sex difference in brain structure. Testosterone – the architect in charge – has obviously been at work here. What will the result of this design difference be? Will it precipitate a boy's brain to operate differently from a girl's brain?

Sex differences in how the brain operates

We know from brain-scanning experiments conducted with children and adolescents that boys' and girls' brains *do* operate in curiously different ways. The brain of a boy is more of a specialist. It tends to delegate certain areas on either one side of the brain or the other to predominantly handle a task. A girl's brain does this, too, but for some tasks it makes use of areas on both sides of the brain to a greater extent than boys' brains do. During verbal tasks, such as judging whether two words rhyme, brain-scans show that there is almost as much activation in girls' right hemispheres as in their left, whereas in boys, left-sided activation is much more pronounced.

It is likely that testosterone-induced changes to brain structure do lead to differences in the way girls' and boys' brains operate. The early enlargement of the speech perception region on the left side in a boy's brain may prepare it for a more one-sided way of operating. Perhaps because it is larger, it will be able to do its job without much aid from its right-sided counterpart. Girls, however, with more equivalently sized right and left brain regions, end up recruiting help from both sides.

For both sexes, though, brain-scanning studies show that the two hemispheres constantly cooperate and interrelate as a seamless whole. For example, although the left-hemisphere speech region is primarily involved in understanding and producing speech, the equivalent right hemisphere region is simultaneously understanding the emotional content of the speech. And within each hemisphere, there is specialization, too. The speech area in the front left of the brain, for instance, is primarily involved not only in the production of speech but also in the understanding of grammatical structure: the use of verbs,

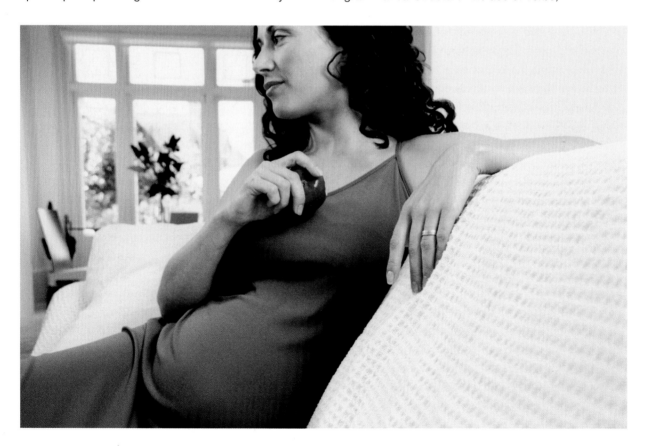

Left and right "crossover"

It is helpful to remember that, irrespective of sex, the left hemisphere controls the *right* side of the body for motor, visual, hearing and sensory tasks (right foot, hand, right visual field, right ear auditory processing, etc.), while the right hemisphere controls the *left* side of the body. This "crossover" also holds true for many – but not all – left-handed people. But boys and girls do differ to begin with, in the pace or sequence in which these patterns become established.

conjunctions and prepositions. The language region farther toward the back of the brain, on the other hand, stores and understands nouns.

Differing sequences of development

Scientists have also discovered that, by the time a baby is born, the right hemisphere of a boy's brain is slightly larger than the left, whereas in girls the two halves of their brains are roughly equal in size.

Is testosterone responsible for causing this difference? When human subjects are tricky to get hold of, scientists tend to conduct experiments on rats instead. It is found that stopping male hormones during a male rat's development results in a female-looking brain with equal halves. On the other hand, raising male hormone levels in female rats makes their brains look more like those of males. Moreover, the results from these animal experiments are confirmed in humans in rare instances where abnormal testosterone levels occur in the womb.

Does this anatomical difference show up in the behavior of the male fetus? There is some suggestion that it does. Male fetuses are about two weeks behind females in moving their mouths (as if doing warm-up speaking exercises) and in turning their heads to hear sounds outside the womb. It's as if, instead of developing the brain cells in its left hemisphere that

How to enhance your son's brain growth before birth

Although both male and female fetuses can benefit from these pre-birth activities, they may provide just the right kind of stimulation for males with their larger right hemispheres and, as we will see, their fewer connections between the two hemispheres.

○ From seven months try playing the same classical music to your baby on a regular basis. (Mozart works well, as it has pronounced patterns.) This will help to speed the development of right-brain spatial skills and increase the likelihood that your child will eventually excel on the sports field!

○ From six or seven months, make a point of singing the same songs to your baby regularly. (A fetus hears its mother's voice best and, next best, deep male voices.) Singing combines a right (music) with a left (words) brain activity and will encourage brain connections between the two halves of your baby's brain to grow.

support speaking and listening skills, the brain of the male fetus has been *temporarily* diverted into spending a little extra time building the brain cells in its right hemisphere – those that will be involved in spatial skills. So, here we have early evidence that testosterone provokes a different *sequence* of brain development. But evidence for boys' early right-hemisphere focus shows up later, in the development of handedness. They are slower than girls to establish a dominant hand, usually the right (which is controlled by the left hemisphere).

1 Effects of testosterone in childhood

The pre-birth surge of testosterone in the male newborn has subsided by the time he is born, down to a low level. But within a few hours, testosterone levels rise dramatically, reaching a peak at two months of age. They then remain at about seventeen times the level found in baby girls until around six months of age, when they rapidly decline. After this time, testosterone levels remain almost as low in boys as in girls all the way through childhood until puberty.

Data on testosterone levels derive from a number of sources, including tables published in 2003 by the University of Utah pathology laboratories (ARUP) showing normal testosterone levels for males and females aged between 0 and 60 (based on thousands of serum collections obtained from all 50 states in the USA).

The baby boy's second surge of testosterone acts once again on the reproductive organs, which is why boy babies often have swollen testicles during this period. But hormonal effects on the brain during this critical time of rapid growth are more permanent. Even at such an early stage, this testosterone boost ensures that the brain of a little boy is irrevocably set on a path of brain development that differs entirely from that of a little girl.

Does brain size make a difference?

From birth to adulthood, the most obvious difference between male brains and female brains is the difference in overall size. Even when the differences between height and weight are taken into account, males have brains that are about 7–8 percent larger than those of females.

The second surge of testosterone that boys' brains experience during infancy probably reinforces this sex difference, one that began months ago in the womb. There is some debate as to why boys' brains are bigger and research efforts are still ongoing, but it may be that boys' heavier bones and muscles need a larger "computer" to run them.

Bigger brain, bigger intellect?

Does this extra brain volume translate to more intelligence? It seems that the answer might be yes, at least when it comes to one particular department. Boys, as young as two and a half, who hear best and most consistently with their left ears (which incidentally reflects the fact that the right side of their brains are better developed and more dominant than the left) will score highly on spatial tests.

This makes sense for two reasons. It is known that the right hemisphere of the brain is primarily in charge of spatial abilities, and it is thought that the brain size differences between the sexes is partly due to boys having larger right hemispheres (see page 13).

Spatial ability involves the ability to remember and analyze spatial relations, such as those required when navigating a maze or mentally manipulating 3-D shapes in space. At the age of three, boys with equivalent vocabulary scores to little girls of the same age are significantly better on spatial tests involving the transforming or rotating of shapes or, for example, using wooden blocks to build a replica of a block-constructed castle or fort. In fact, at all ages, spatial skills are one area where sex differences are largest and most consistent. Boys do seem to be smarter than girls in this area.

And what about "tomboys"?

There exist rare cases in which baby girls are exposed to higher than normal amounts of testosterone in utero. Although surgery can correct the masculinized sex organs, the effects on the brain are permanent. These little girls act like little boys, enjoy rough physical play, are more competitive and choose the kinds of toys that little boys prefer. When carefully observed, these girls consistently choose construction and transport toys (thought to attract baby boys more because of their visual-spatial features, moving parts, potential for assembly and dismantling) and, like many boys (with their slightly larger right hemispheres), they have higher than average spatial abilities.

How to spur your young son's brain growth

Enhance overall brain potential by taking into account the natural sequence in which boys' brains develop, then speed up the sequence. Right-hemisphere regions are favored over left to begin with, so, early on, encourage and accelerate the development of right-hemisphere skills. (Gifted boys, with extremely high overall intelligence, often are found to have very strong right-hemisphere skills that were encouraged *from an early age*.)

○ Encourage play with a variety of construction and transport toys.

○ Provide plenty of opportunity for your son to play with sand, water or other substances and containers of all sizes and shapes.

○ Encourage safe explorations of the spaces surrounding him, indoors and outdoors.

○ From birth, or before, expose your son to music. As early as he seems interested, teach him how to play a musical instrument.

Supplement right-hemisphere activities with those that encourage both left-brain and right-brain development. Expose your son to plenty of finger-plays, nursery rhymes, action songs, singing and moving around to music.

Brain structure and operational differences

Research is only just beginning to reveal the structural and operating differences between boys' and girls' brains. Two are of particular interest as their effects on behavior are seen in childhood.

The "tiger" in boys' tanks

Scientists have known for some time that a primitive collection of brain cells deep within the brain is bigger in male rats than in female rats. With the aid of brain-scanning involving children as young as four, scientists have now measured the size of a similar structure in humans – known as the amygdala – and found a similar sex difference.

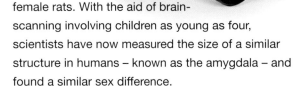

The testosterone surge during infancy appears to enlarge the amygdala, making it visibly bigger in boys' brains. Evidence suggests, though, that this enlargement occurs with the first surge of testosterone in the male fetus and that subsequent testosterone levels influence its size throughout life.

For many years Esso (later Texaco) used the popular slogan to "put a tiger in your tank" to give your car added energy and zoom. This enlarged amygdala (still a relatively tiny almond-shaped structure) is, essentially, the "tiger in a boy's tank."

Only very recently, researchers were fascinated to discover that at just three months old boys seemed able to distinguish between male and female babies of the same age. Three-month-old girls, on the other hand, were entirely oblivious to this difference. The researchers suggested that the high levels of testosterone boy babies experience during this period may have heightened their awareness. They speculated whether this stemmed from testosterone-fueled growth of this primitive, sex-attuned structure, the tiny "tiger" deep within their brains.

This structure is known to influence instinctive sexual behavior and emotional arousal. It is likely to be the part of the brain responsible for the different behavior of boys and girls that parents can't help noticing. Somehow, boys do tend to make their presence a little more felt – they often appear to be more active, curious, competitive, territorial and aggressive than girls. From an early age, they engage in, and enjoy, more rough-and-tumble play.

Connecting the two halves

A structure in the brain that has attracted a substantial amount of research, as well as some heated debate, is what might be called the brain's central connecting bridge; its proper name is the corpus callosum.

This "bridge" comprises a thick bundle of branching pathways of nerve cells and fibers that connect the two sides of the brain like an extensive motorway system, with information traveling in both directions. These neural networks carry electrical signals, allowing the two sides of the brain to talk to each other.

Some research is revealing that, even allowing for males' larger brain size, specific parts of this structure appear to be significantly *thicker* in adult females. And in 2001, a team of Israeli scientists discovered that this central connector is also thicker in unborn females. In children, though, sex differences in the size or volume of this structure have not been entirely confirmed, although it certainly *looks* different. In young boys its shape is long and tubular; in girls it is more bulbous toward the end nearer the back of the brain, the part that corresponds to the thicker part in adult women.

The thicker part of a female corpus callosum is in the area concerned with language and may explain why girls tend to outperform boys in some verbal skills. During reading, for example, areas in both hemispheres are active in girls' brains, but boys' processing is almost entirely one-sided.

Sex differences in the corpus callosum

	BOYS	GIRLS
Appearance	longer, thinner	more bulbous
Function	inhibits cross-talk between the hemispheres	enhances cross-talk between the hemispheres
Side effects	less growth of cross-over neural pathways	more growth of cross-over neural pathways
	specialized, unilateral brain cell growth occurs more	shared, bilateral brain cell growth occurs more
Net result	better at some tasks (mathematical and spatial) earlier than girls	better at some tasks (social and verbal) earlier than boys

LOCATION OF THE CORPUS CALLOSUM
(the central connecting bridge between the two hemispheres)

top view
(top half of the brain removed)

front

corpus callosum

back

side view
(mid-section)

front

back

corpus callosum

Cross-talk between the hemispheres

Hormones may affect how the corpus callosum "bridge" operates. It is thought that male hormones may cause it to inhibit or filter out cross-talk between the hemispheres. The growth of interconnecting "motorways" is discouraged in some instances, with the result that boys' way of thinking tends to be somewhat single-minded! In boys' brains this rather bossy connector behaves a bit like a bouncer who wants to keep people apart. The male brain likes to make logical, rational decisions in the left zone, say, without having to contend with interference from the more irrational, emotional right zone.

In contrast, female hormones act on this connecting bridge in girls to facilitate interhemispheric chitchat, encouraging the growth of "motorways" connecting left and right zones. When girls are trying to make a decision, they can more easily draw on both their emotional right and logical left sides.

Specialize for success

In boys, the connector's blocking mechanisms may result in an increase in specialized regions. Boys' brains do become more highly developed on the right side, and if this specialization is carried to the extreme in some individuals, one might predict that among the world's most gifted mathematicians and chess players, there would be more males. And this is indeed the case. Unlike those of average ability, boys gifted in mathematics show almost no activity in the left brain when working on problems.

So, even though boys' brains may have a system that appears to slow down development in some areas compared with girls, the one-sided specialization that their brains then dive into may mean that their potential to surpass girls in certain areas is increased.

Differing sequences of childhood brain development

As well as having brains that differ in structure compared with girls' brains, the order in which boys begin developing and using various parts of their brains also differs. In boys, structures located in the right hemisphere are more often activated to begin with, whereas in girls, the opposite pattern occurs.

In 1990, evidence that boys' and girls' brains follow a different sequence of development from an early age was provided by scientists Janet and David Shucard.

Words and music

When adults listen to music they mostly activate the right hemisphere of their brain, whereas speech and words is mainly the domain of regions in the left hemisphere. The Shucards wanted to see how babies' brains processed these different types of information.

They recorded the electrical activity in the brains of three-month-old infants while they were listening either to stories or to music. They found that, irrespective of whether baby boys heard words or music, most of the electrical activity in their brains occurred on the *right* side. But when the Shucards looked at what was going on in girl babies' brains, they found that when girls heard either words or music, it was the *left* side of their brains that became more excited.

When the babies were six months old the researchers tested them again, and the results were almost the same – the *right* hemispheres of boy babies, and the *left* hemispheres of girl babies were most responsive to both kinds of stimuli.

IQ tests

It is hard to measure intelligence in a way that is fair to both sexes. Psychologists have tried to figure this out, tinkering with intelligence quotient (IQ) tests for years.

The most widely used measure is Weschler's intelligence scales (WISC). There are eleven sub-tests, of which only two reveal similar scores for males and females. Males score higher than females on six of the remaining nine (masculine-type) sub-tests; females score higher than males on the other three (feminine-type) sub-tests. Amazingly, these sex differences are substantially confirmed across cultures.

The results demonstrate not only how different the brains of males and females are, but the extent to which scores depend on the chosen tests. Many original sub-tests had to be omitted by Weschler because they so strongly favored one or the other sex.

In all, over 30 sub-tests had to be eliminated. One test, which involved mentally navigating through a maze, favored boys so overwhelmingly that psychologists pondered for a time whether girls' brains were totally without a "spatial factor"!

However, that wasn't the end of the story. To their surprise, they discovered that some of the babies were beginning to use the "correct" part of their brains for the different kinds of stimuli. Some of the boy babies, for example, were beginning to show a more pronounced left-hemisphere response to the words, and some of the girl babies were starting to use their right hemispheres more in response to hearing the music.

So, it seems that the brains of boy and girl babies are headed for roughly the same ultimate destination, but that the different hormones (which flood their brains) dictate the particular route, or sequence of events, they must follow to get there.

1 Testosterone and the teenager

The third, and final, surge of testosterone in a boy's life occurs with the onset of puberty. Over a four- or five-year period, beginning about the age of twelve, testosterone levels rise dramatically (see page 12). As before, such soaring hormone levels have very obvious effects on sexual reproductive organs, but they also have less obvious but profound effects inside the brain.

As happened during previous periods of testosterone rises, there are noticeable effects on the sexual reproductive system. Boys' sexual organs grow larger and secondary sex characteristics (deepening of the voice, growth of facial and body hair) make their appearance. But, as before, the brain does not escape the powerful influence of this male hormone.

Adolescent growth

Scientists were excited to discover, only recently, that the brain continues to build itself throughout the teenage years and into early adulthood.

In general terms, the brain matures from its base (the brainstem) upward, and from the frontal regions to those at the back. In puberty, it now looks as though hormones initiate another period of intensive growth in the upper frontal region of the brain. This is one of the last areas of brain to *begin* "wiring" up in childhood, at around the age of three (see page 150) and is, in evolutionary terms, the "newest" part of the brain. The frontal regions of the brain deal with planning,

forethought and other more "intellectual" functions.

Scientists were surprised to find that the brain continues to grow in this region during adolescence and does not complete its work until the late twenties or beyond for males (earlier for females). And, still in specialist mode, the male brain grows a larger *left* frontal region relative to the right, whereas for females each side develops to a similar size.

The excitable tiger

Once again, as it did earlier in life, testosterone makes the "tiger" (or amygdala), the brain's center of emotional arousal and excitement, grow even bigger in boys' brains at this time. By adulthood, the male amygdala ends up being 16 percent larger than the female's. Neural pathways from this structure lead upward and forward into the region around the eyes and under the forehead. This higher, connecting region that is in charge of complex thinking skills, and planning and executing ideas, is involved in monitoring behavior and controlling aggression. Compared with teenage girls, boys have a smaller amount of this controlling region in relation to the impulsive, excitable "tiger" (see page 18). This difference means that girls at this age are better equipped than boys to censor their angry and aggressive urges.

There is further discussion about the effects of this third surge of testosterone on how it affects teenage boys' thinking and behavior in Chapter 7 (see pages 150–151).

Comparing the brains of adolescent boys and girls

A research team at Harvard Medical School wanted to find out if males and females differed in their frontal brain development and therefore in the degree of self-control over emotional behavior. Using magnetic resonance imaging (MRI), they examined how the brains of males and females responded while viewing photographs of faces expressing fear. They concluded there was indeed a sex difference in the rate at which brain circuits linking the amygdala (the "tiger") with the pre-frontal cortex region matured.

With age, adolescent girls showed a progressive increase in frontal, relative to amygdala, activation, whereas males failed to show a significant age-related difference. Other research confirms the Harvard findings and suggests that the brains of males may not be fully mature in this department until their late twenties.

1 Building a boy's brain

We have seen that, although boys' and girls' brains grow in roughly the same way, the presence of that all-important chemical – testosterone – at particular stages in a boy's life alters the timing as to when, and the sequence in which, different brain regions experience exuberant growth spurts. At what level do these differences lie? Is it right down at the cellular level or is it more wrapped up with the brain's circuitry? Science does have some of the answers.

One way in which neuroscientists determine how brain construction of boys differs from that of girls is to investigate and examine which neural networks mature the earliest.

The birth of neural networks

Nerve cells (or *neurons*) are produced in the fetus at the mind-boggling rate of 250,000 per minute. And this is only the average over the nine months of pregnancy; the rate is actually much faster at certain periods as most neurons are already in place within the first four months of gestation.

At birth, your baby's brain has its full complement of 100 billion neurons. However, they are very poorly connected – imagine billions of people, each person with thousands of telephones, but virtually none of the phones hooked up!

At first, the neurons are mere saplings, but they soon begin to grow a substantial number of "roots" (to *receive* messages from other neurons) and a "trunk" that develops "branches" (to *send* messages to other neurons). The communication point between two neurons (where the branches of one neuron and the roots of another "talk") is called a *synapse*.

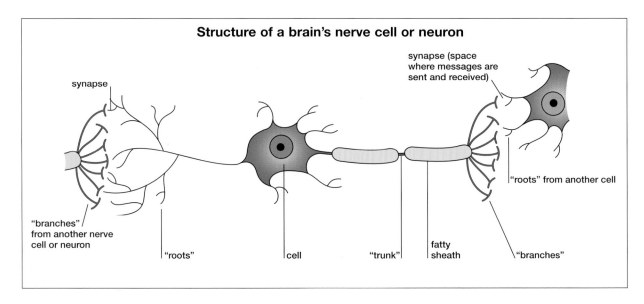

Structure of a brain's nerve cell or neuron

synapse

synapse (space where messages are sent and received)

"roots" from another cell

"branches" from another nerve cell or neuron

"roots"

cell

"trunk"

fatty sheath

"branches"

At peak growth, some 15,000 synapses may develop on the branches of every neuron. In order to accommodate them all, more branches have to grow to increase the surface area. Synapses are known to increase at an astonishing rate of 2 million every second. It takes a lot of power to run that many connections. No wonder babies sleep a lot!

These neural networks – comprising billions of neurons with trillions of branches and their synapses – continue to grow, like a rapidly thickening forest seen on fast-forwarded film, throughout the first and into the second year of life. Everything your baby sees, hears, smells, tastes or touches translates into electrical activity in the brain, increasing the chance of a particular neural network or collection of synapses surviving and being made permanent.

Forging permanent networks

When the "trunk" of a neuron is frequently activated (by repeated experience), it begins to form an insulation of white encasing material (see Those little gray cells…, right). By examining the amount of white matter in boys' and girls' brains, neuroscientists can determine the order in which different brain regions develop, and which ones are maturing the earliest.

Some areas of the nervous system mature quickly, whereas others continue refining themselves well past puberty. The first part of the brain to develop permanent networks in both boys and girls is the area involving the inner ear; it controls balance and coordination and tells the body where it is in space. Amazingly, some of these networks begin to insulate themselves (that is, turn white with their myelin coating) just twelve weeks after fertilization.

Other regions to show some white matter early in fetal development are the motor areas of the brain (relating to voluntary movements), the hearing centers and part of the brain involved in vision. The neural networks related to sense of smell are well insulated at birth, and those related to touch are fully insulated by six months after birth.

Did you know...?
A child's brain doubles in weight during the first three years. This weight increase is almost entirely due to the proliferation of synapses – literally trillions of connecting points.

Those little gray cells...
Boys' brains have more *white* matter and girls' brains have more *gray*. What do these terms mean?

White matter When neuroscientists study brain-scans, part of the neural networks show up as white. These are the well-established nerve fibers or "trunks" that send messages over long distances to different parts of the brain and body. With repeated use, they become covered in a white fatty substance called myelin (from the Latin for "bark"). This myelin acts like insulation, stopping "leaks" and cross-talk between other "trunks." Best of all, once this coating is in place, brain signals can travel 100 times faster!

Gray matter What shows up on scans as gray areas are where the brain cells without long white trunks are packed closely together. (They look darker when densely packed because their cell centers are faintly gray, but in reality "gray cells" are not gray at all, but pink!) Agatha Christie's detective, Monsieur Poirot, was right about one thing, though: the gray cells are where all the concentrated thinking takes place. They do the local processing, while neurons with long white trunks provide long-distance communication between different gray matter areas.

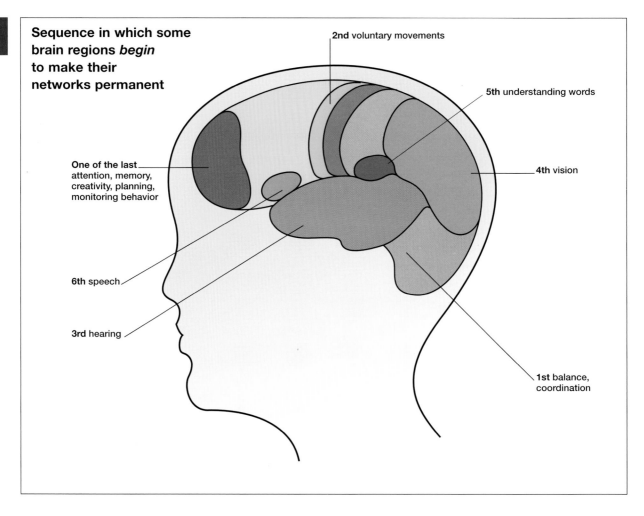

Sequence in which some brain regions *begin* to make their networks permanent

2nd voluntary movements

5th understanding words

One of the last attention, memory, creativity, planning, monitoring behavior

4th vision

6th speech

3rd hearing

1st balance, coordination

Some important areas in the higher (less primitive, more recently evolved) parts of the brain begin to mature later. The frontal region of the brain, in charge of complex functions – attending, planning, creativity, impulse control and behavior regulation – has an initial phase of growth between the ages of three and six years, followed by another much later growth phase during adolescence.

Although the neural networks involved with basic sensory and motor functions develop in roughly the same *sequence* in boys' and girls' brains, some mature earlier in one sex or the other.

Unique to males, from birth to about age six, specialized networks associated with visual-spatial discrimination, gross motor movements, visual targeting and recalling information receive concentrated attention.

Windows of opportunity

Another way of determining how brains develop is to look at which different regions of the brain show the most rapid growth – where the most synapses or connecting points are being produced. In this case, neuroscientists look for areas of dense gray matter.

In young brains, scientists don't have far to look. The huge overproduction of synapses that occurs in children's brains during the first four or five years marks the onset of all sorts of new abilities. Different parts of the brain overproduce synapses at different times. These are the times when it is easier for your son to learn new things rapidly.

Some of these "windows of opportunity" remain open for a very short time before the most used networks begin to insulate (or myelinate) their "trunks." The connections for sight must be developed within the first few months, for example, and the first five years are the prime time for learning new languages.

It is during these sensitive periods that the brain has to make decisions about which synapses to keep and which ones to eliminate. Those synaptic connections stimulated often enough will become insulated and permanent, whereas those connections not used enough will be "pruned" away. As neuroscientists are fond of saying, "Those connections that fire together, wire together!"

By looking at when grey matter is at its most dense, which indicates a particularly huge number of synapses or connections, neuroscientists have gained some understanding of when these sensitive periods occur, although there is still a lot that is not known and research continues. The table (see right) highlights some differences as to when these critical periods take place for boys and for girls.

The "pruning" process

A child's brain produces vastly more synapses than it will ever need. Only the "fittest" (in this case, the ones receiving most electrical signals or stimulation) will survive. These more active synapses essentially tell the brain, "Keep me!" These routes through the brain will then become permanent fixtures.

The synapses that are rarely activated – perhaps those that would enable your son to become a famous musician, a fluent speaker of Chinese or a trapeze artist – wither away. In fact, between infancy and adolescence, your baby will be losing an average of 20 billion synapses per day! But don't worry! This elimination process is actually very beneficial. With less interference from competing "lines," the neural networks run much more smoothly.

Although both boys' and girls' brains are "pruned" in this way, the resulting neural networks end up looking so different for each sex, it's as if they were designed by two different architects. Eventually, boys' brains end up with more "trunk" lines, and girls' brains end up with more synapses and "branches."

Sensitive periods in brain development

	BOYS	GIRLS
BALANCE		
Peak in synapses	6–12 months	6–12 months
End of critical period	2½ years	2½ years
MOTOR		
Peak in synapses	Several peaks from fetus to late childhood	
End of critical period	young adult	young adult
HEARING		
Peak in synapses	3 months to 12 years	3 months to 12 years
End of critical period	12+ years	12+ years
VISION		
Peak in synapses	3–7 months	2–6 months
End of critical period	6 months to 8 years	6 months to 8 years
LANGUAGE		
Peak in synapses	9 months to 2+ years	8 months to 2+ years
End of critical period	6–7 years	6–7 years
ATTENTION, PLANNING		
1st peak in synapses	2½–7 years	2½–7 years
2nd peak in synapses	17–27 years	14–24 years
End of critical period	late twenties	mid-twenties

1 Nurture: the critical difference

How much difference can you make in your son's intellectual potential? Generally speaking, genes and hormones are responsible for the basic wiring plan of a boy's brain. Experience, however, helps to fine-tune the brain's connections. And it's also this experience that helps his brain adapt its structure to a particular environment (the culture, family, school, peer group).

Stimulating environmental input can actually alter the structure of the brain at every age, including very old age. (And, incidentally, this phenomenon applies to the brains of *humans*. No longer is it solely applicable to the brains of snails, rats and other animals upon which neuroscientists often focus.)

The greatest changes are brought about during the period when the brain is growing most rapidly – the first ten years. At no other time will learning be so rapid. By the age of two, the brains of children have as many synapses as adult brains do, and brain-scans show that between the ages of three and ten they have

Q **Are there any foods that will boost my son's brain growth?**

A The single most important nutritional choice mothers can make to increase the IQ of a child of either sex is to breast-feed. Breast-fed children score an average eight points higher on IQ tests given at the age of eight. The longer a mother breast-feeds during the first year, the higher the child's IQ. Perhaps these points are linked to two findings: first, the longer babies are breast-fed the sooner they reach various developmental milestones; and, second, the fewer ear infections they contract (see pages 80–81).

Q **What is the most important thing I can do to enhance my son's brain development?**

A From the beginning, providing warm, loving touch is the most important way to "grow" any baby's brain. It may be especially important to boys, though, since from birth they are less sensitive to touch than girls. Research shows that babies deprived of this type of sensory and social stimulation end up stunted in every sense – emotionally, physically, and intellectually. So, touching your baby is one of the best, and easiest, ways to make a real difference in your son's mental and emotional development.

twice as many. There is no doubt that providing your son with interesting and challenging experiences during these years in particular can boost the growth of his "little gray cells" and, in turn, the white matter a tremendous amount.

Stimulating experiences

From birth, the diameter of the semi-circular canals in the inner ear (part of the balance system) is larger in boys than girls. Because boys are more prone to ear infections and these can affect the development of the balance system, the following study may have special relevance for parents of boys.

Researchers wanted to investigate if stimulation could make a difference to the development of babies' inner ears and balance centers. They exposed babies, ranging in age from three to thirteen months, to sixteen sessions of chair spinning. Four times a week for four weeks, the babies were seated on a researcher's lap and spun around ten times in a swivel chair. Each spin was followed by an abrupt stop.

To maximize the stimulation, the babies were spun in different directions and held in three different positions. Needless to say the babies absolutely loved this treatment! During the rest periods between each spin, they became impatient for more!

Another group of babies sat on the researcher's lap during each session, but they did not get the "fairground" spinning treatment.

The results were remarkable. The babies who were spun were more advanced in their reflexes and motor skills. At the end of the study, one four-month-old "spinning" twin had mastered head control and could sit independently, whereas his unstimulated twin brother had only just begun to hold his head up.

As far as stimulating experiences are concerned, though, probably the greatest intellectual advance in a boy's or a girl's brain development is learning to talk, the subject of the next chapter.

Ringing the changes

Introducing variety into your young child's life is key to accelerating brain growth.

○ Numbers of toys matter less than variety. Rotate different toys and play materials every week or so.

○ Remove toys *before* your child becomes too used to them. When they reappear later, they will suddenly be fascinating again!

○ Move toys to another location to give them novelty value (and for boys, in particular, it will help to speed the development of their visual memories).

○ Try to visit different places and people to expand your child's variety of experiences.

○ Provide opportunities for interacting with a variety of people of different ages. (This will especially benefit boys, who are not naturally as social as girls.)

○ Point out different forms of transport and use as many as possible (these hold particular fascination for boys).

○ Arrange as many opportunities as you can for your child to interact with different animals.

○ Involve your son in a variety of household activities that are not stereotypically male: cooking, cleaning, gardening or laundry tasks. In addition, mothers and fathers can adopt non-stereotypical gender roles.

2 how do boys communicate?

2 Language: a natural instinct

Like most parents, Sarah and Rob are exceptionally proud of their beautiful baby boy, and they're thrilled that their little daughter now has someone to play with. But now that he is a year old, they cannot help making comparisons. His older sister was able to say several words by this age. They have heard that boys' language skills may lag behind those of girls, but is this true? Could this be the explanation or could there be something more serious going on?

There is really no need to worry. For most children, whatever their sex, learning to speak a language goes without a snag. When you think of just how difficult it is to master the vocabulary, grammar and syntax of a foreign language, to speak in fluent sentences with the correct intonation and pronunciation, it should come home to you just how striking an achievement it is for a child to learn how to do this, without any formal instruction, and in only a few short years. It should convince you, as it has most linguists, that human language is an instinct, a built-in behavior that is just as natural as eating and sleeping.

At the same time, language is the key to bringing out the best in all children. It is
○ fundamental to all learning,
○ vital for communicating with others,
○ an invaluable aid to social and emotional well-being.

So it is perhaps not surprising that parents do worry, especially if their son or daughter seems less advanced than a sibling, or a friend's or neighbor's child of the same age.

Parents inevitably make comparisons. And talking is such a basic part of life, parents' interest will always be caught by reports, statistics or rumors that relate to the development of children's speech and general communication abilities.

This chapter looks at the way in which young children learn to communicate, how their brains build

the neural networks that are involved in the various forms of communication and the brain development that takes place before and after birth. It looks at some common perceptions – that boys begin speaking later than girls, that speech difficulties are common among boys, that social class makes a difference – and explains what you can do to encourage and enhance your son's verbal skills.

A major brain-building project

Unlike all other mammals, humans have evolved the ability to communicate through language. It's as if they have an extra computer chip in their brains. But even though all babies are biologically primed for language, learning to speak probably still represents one of the most sensational intellectual achievements of any person's life.

Infants have to start, of course, at a relatively rudimentary level. Their brains are not adequately developed to produce speech at birth. Some of the

neural circuits for *hearing* language, however, begin to mature in the fetus's brain as early as 24 weeks (see page 25), and by the time a baby is born, a functional auditory system – one that is especially primed to hear human voices – has developed. It is after birth, however, that the bulk of the work toward learning a language takes place.

Complex circuits in the brain have to be built before a baby can even begin to make sense of single words. Building these neural networks depends on hearing literally millions of speech sounds and words in just the first year alone.

It's lucky, then, that development in other areas of the brain is already well under way at birth. Some of the earliest networks to form are those controlling the five senses: smell, touch, taste, vision and hearing. Everything a baby touches, smells, tastes and sees will help him make sense of the speech sounds his brain hears and begins to categorize.

2 Stepping-stones to language development

Many people believe that girls are more advanced than boys when it comes to the development of language. But, is this just a popular misconception or is it actually the case? Do their brains develop according to a different sequence so that it just *seems* as if the girls are ahead? From the beginning, boys and girls interact with the world in different ways, and that may explain the differences.

At birth, all the information babies learn about their world comes to them through their senses. Everything that a baby learns through touching, tasting, smelling, seeing and hearing is a stepping-stone toward the ability to communicate not only non-verbally, but verbally as well. Research shows that these early learning experiences actually alter brain structure. But does the pace or order of learning on the road to language differ for girls and boys?

Smell

The sense of smell is the most developed of a baby's abilities at birth. Studies show that the mother's scent makes a baby's movements more organized and calm. However, research has established that from the first day of life sex differences in smell exist.

In one experiment, one-day-old baby girls were found to turn their heads to smell a new odor, but when the new odors were presented to boy babies of the same age, it did not affect their head-turning behavior. Other experiments have established that at different ages throughout life, females are more sensitive to smells. But since it is also known that testosterone decreases olfactory sensitivity, these findings are perhaps not surprising.

Olfactory experience is important to the newborn nutritionally (babies can smell their mother's milk), emotionally (familiar smells engender a sense of security) and cognitively (babies start to recognize and remember odors). But whatever sex differences exist, they appear to be quite small. In one study, for instance, boys aged three were just as adept as girls in correctly identifying the odor of their own sibling (T-shirt sniffing was involved).

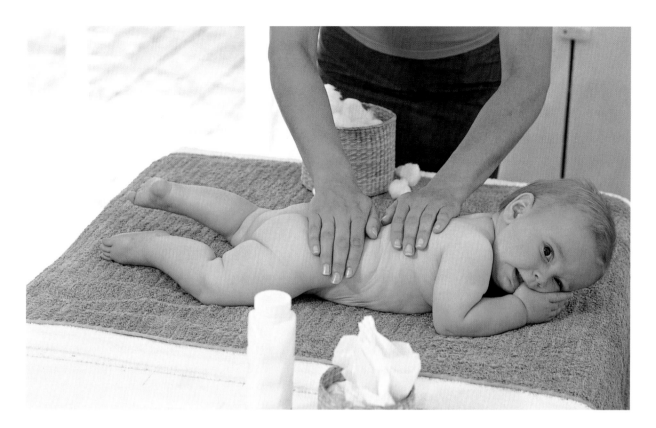

Touch

The sense of touch is also one of the more advanced abilities of newborns. Experiments show that by three months of age, babies can tell the difference between a smooth or bumpy object (using their hands and, of course, their mouths!). But once again, there is an early difference between the boys and the girls.

Newborn girls tend to be more sensitive to the lightest touches on most parts of their bodies compared with boys. Although it is doubtful these sex differences would have much impact on language development in the long term, plenty of touch is indeed important. Touch does seem to facilitate brain growth in important language-related areas: in one study, four-month-old babies given an eight-minute massage before performing a task (one designed to assess early memory and sensory discrimination skills) were significantly better at the task than babies who were not given the massage treatments.

In a study involving six-year-olds, boys were found to be far more sensitive to touch on the right sides of their bodies than the left sides. This ties in with the research in Chapter 1 (see pages 15 and 20), showing that it is about this age that boys' brains are shifting toward more dedicated *left*-hemisphere growth (and so the opposite side of the body becomes dominant for touch). The girls were more symmetrical in their touch sensitivity, reflecting their right-hemisphere growth and more bilateral functioning.

Many other scientific experiments have demonstrated the emotional benefits of early, loving touch to a baby. At this time, touch operates to reduce stress hormones in the bloodstream and, at the same time, the immune system is given a boost. And, of course, under these "ideal" conditions babies' brains can devote most of their energy to building the neural networks and connections that will support emerging language abilities.

Taste

Some research suggests that females tend to have lower thresholds for detecting sweet, sour and salty tastes. Perhaps the important thing, though, is that both male and female babies have a preference for sweet tastes, predisposing them to prefer the taste of that high "IQ elixir," their mother's milk (see page 28).

Because babies are able to taste the flavors in the amniotic fluid that surrounds them before birth, the familiar tastes found in their mother's milk after birth create an immediate bond. For both boys and girls, social, emotional and intellectual development is accelerated by these early taste sensations.

Vision

Newborns can see only what is 8–15 inches (20–40 cm) directly in front of them. They can detect different light levels, shapes and movements, but by and large, what they see is pretty fuzzy. With exposure to stimulating sights and scenes in the first few months, however, the visual system develops rapidly. By three months infants can discriminate between colors, and by eight months their vision is as good as an adult's.

It is thought that the raised testosterone levels during the first six months of a boy's life, however, are responsible for some minor sex differences. Boys are slower to develop two visual skills during this period: binocularity (coordinating both eyes) and hyperacuity (detecting very fine detail). Differences are not obvious

in newborns and virtually disappear by six months. In fact, later on, boys outperform girls in some visual skills. As young as three, boys' visual-spatial skills involving the mental rotation of objects in space are found to be significantly better than those of girls.

Looking at the world

Another curious visually related ability is found to differ between girls and boys (see box opposite). This may help to explain some behavioral differences between boys and girls that are clearly observable during the first year of life.

Boys show more interest than girls in their global surroundings, in exploring the space around them. Quick as a flash they will empty your cupboards and drawers, or topple that nice stack of folded laundry. Not only do they love exploring space, but they don't mind rearranging it for you as well! Girls, on the other hand, seem more inclined to attend to the details of people or objects in their immediate environment.

The earlier development of binocularity and hyperacuity in girls' vision may predispose the sexes to behave in these different ways. One would predict, therefore, that girls (whose skills in these areas develop earlier) would be more inclined to find the visual details of things increasingly fascinating because they come into sharper focus.

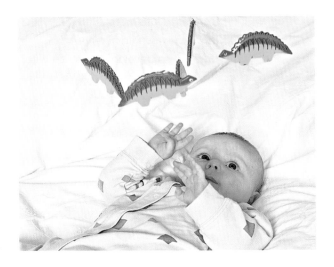

Matching the shapes

In 1996, scientists at the University of California's School of Medicine found that when asked whether B or C was more like A, boys as young as four tended to choose B, the figure with the same overall shape but with different internal elements. Girls chose C.

At this early age, boys' *right*, but girls' left, hemispheres undergo concentrated development. This explains why boys chose figure B. Their brains focused on the overall global shape (right-hemisphere processing) while the girls focused on the details within the overall shape (left-hemisphere processing).

After about the age of six, however, boys' brains shift to increasing growth of left-hemisphere sites, while girls' brains grow more neural networks and connections not only in the right hemisphere, but also *between* the two hemispheres. This helps to explain why older boys and girls in this study were both increasingly likely to choose B and yet why girls were never as global in their approach as boys. At twelve, boys chose B almost 80 percent of the time, whereas girls chose it only 50 percent of the time.

Children were asked to select which of the two figures – B or C – was most like the first one (A).

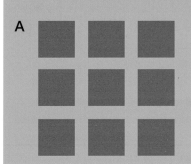 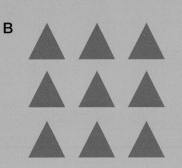 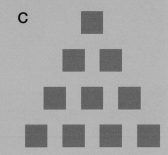

But why are little boys fascinated with objects that dive and zoom – with toy cars, planes, trains, balls and anything that can be turned into a projectile? This, too, may come down to an interesting difference in the order in which visual abilities develop. In a study that measured the brain waves of children from two months of age to sixteen years, it was discovered that boys' brains really go to town between two months and six years in developing the neural networks for *visually tracking* objects. Astonishingly, girls' brains do not appear to make a serious start on these networks until the age of eight!

Research from the University of Cambridge in the UK has now provided evidence that sex differences in vision and brain development are indeed related to testosterone levels. And this research revealed the following prenatal as well as postnatal effects:

○ Twenty-four hours after birth, boy infants looked longer at an inanimate mechanical mobile (right-hemisphere processing) than girls did, while the female babies looked longer at a human face (left-hemisphere processing).

○ The more fetal testosterone a baby boy produced *before* birth (measured in the amniotic fluid), the less eye contact he made at twelve months (showing slower left-hemisphere development).

○ The higher the amniotic fluid testosterone levels pre-birth, the smaller the vocabulary (left-hemisphere development) at eighteen months in both males and females.

Hearing

Because vision is quite poor at birth, hearing provides babies with their first access to the world beyond their reach. Babies are insensitive to quiet sounds but have a special ability to perceive the sounds of human speech. In fact, in their first year, babies are more attuned than they will ever be again to the speech sounds of *any* language.

Because we use language as the main means of teaching our children, hearing may be the most important of all the senses to your son's intellectual future. Although the sexes differ in the degree to which their left hemispheres favor language, in normal circumstances boys hear the sounds of language as well as girls do. As Chapter 1 explains (see page 13), one language region of the brain is larger on the left than the right side of the brain in males; and during certain language tasks there is more left-brain activity in males, compared with females, whose patterns of activity are more bilateral.

Listening from the womb

Like most people you might assume that the fetus hears only a confusion of sounds, the mother's heartbeat, the whooshing of fluids and loud sounds from the world outside. But this belief was shattered in 1986 with a number of startling experiments.

Researchers found that fetuses can "recognize"

- ○ familiar phrases (Mothers repeating several times a day the words, "Hello, baby, how are you today?" soon provoked slower heartbeats in their fetuses when saying these words.)
- ○ familiar music (The theme songs from soap operas that mothers-to-be in Ireland listened to were of particular interest to their babies once they were born. When the music was played, the babies' heartbeats slowed as a response.)
- ○ familiar syllables (After hearing the English word "baby" several times through a loudspeaker pressed to the mother's pregnant tummy, French babies began to pay attention and their heart rates slowed. Eventually, this response stopped: the baby was bored with the word "baby." But when the syllables were reversed to "bee-bay," the effects were seen again and their heart rates slowed once more.)
- ○ a familiar children's story (Newborns' sucking was faster and longer in response to stories they had previously heard only in the womb.)
- ○ their mother's voice. (Newborns can distinguish their own mother's voice from other female voices even though they have previously heard her speak and laugh only from the watery environment of the womb.)

Baby talk

Although many a parent might vow never to use that silly baby talk to *their* child, somehow, when the time comes, it seems like the best way of talking. This is because people instinctively sense that babies can hear better if they speak louder, more slowly and with lots of intonation and expression. And they do! Experiments show that babies suck faster if their mothers talk in a highly inflected higher-pitched voice rather than a low and monotone one.

The mystery of the tasty toys

In 2000, California researchers Roberts and Bell wanted to investigate whether eight-month-old boys and girls would attend to a novel toy for the same amount of time and also if it made any difference whether they were seated on their mother's lap or in an infant chair. Each child was given four toys, each one for 60 seconds, or until they had dropped the toy three times.

A surprising sex difference was revealed. The boy babies spent an overall greater percentage of time sucking or tasting the toy, whereas the little girls spent more time on visual inspection. (Perhaps less surprisingly, both sexes spent more time with the toy in their mouths if they were seated on their mother's lap.)

What could explain these differences? Was it just that the boys preferred taste and touch (via the mouth) as their favorite channels to find out about their world, and the girls preferred touch (mainly via hands) and vision?

At this age, boys are more adept at seeing global

shapes, and girls are three or four weeks ahead of boys at discerning finer detail. Did these different visual strengths influence their approach to exploring?

Boys at this age give priority to synapse-building in the back regions of the brain (which are responsible for attending to general, spatial aspects of the environment) over the front regions (which are responsible for more concentrated and specific attending). In girls, the reverse is true. Perhaps these different developmental timetables explain the babies' behavior.

Girls' brains prefer to build connections in the regions controlling fine motor movement before developing the gross motor regions. Boys' brains have the opposite preference. Putting the toys in their mouths may have been the more natural kind of movement at that stage for boys, whereas finer manipulation came more naturally to the girls.

Of course, it could be that the boys, with their less discerning taste buds, simply needed more time to realize that the toy didn't taste that great, nor did it produce any milk! Without further research, it's difficult to come to a firm conclusion.

2 Are boys less verbal?

We have seen that babies use all their senses to help them learn about their world. These sensory experiences are vital not only for learning how to communicate non-verbally, but also for helping them to understand and learn how to produce speech. Speech is, without doubt, the most important form of stimulation a baby receives. Every vowel and consonant babies hear is critical for shaping their neural networks in their brains that will be involved in helping them to understand and to produce language.

Language ability develops rapidly during the first two years, following a similar time schedule for both sexes. From birth, baby boys and girls are fascinated by their mother's face and move in rhythm with her speech (although boys find mobiles engrossing as well!). Although both sexes are adept at recognizing their mother's voice, University of Cambridge research suggests that hormones may affect early language development. At eighteen months, babies whose prenatal testosterone levels had been higher were found to have smaller vocabularies. Most girls were talking before the boys, but prenatal testosterone levels affected girls' language development, too.

Babbling

Babies begin making their first vowel sounds (oohs and aahs) at about two months of age, and babbling in earnest, with a number of consonant sounds as part of the repertoire, at about four to five months. By the end of the first year, English-speaking babies generally will have mastered most of the vowels and about half the consonants. Although some degree of this progress depends on the maturation of their vocal machinery, it is equally affected by stimulation.

The more attention parents pay to their baby's babbling and the more they imitate and respond, the more their baby will learn and babble back. Curiously, one study found that mothers of boys tail off in their verbal encouragements during the period between four and eight months, whereas mothers of girls continue to talk to their babies just as much as they ever did. (See page 46 for more on these findings.)

Understanding words

By nine or ten months, most babies begin to link words with their meaning. Experiments show that babies of both sexes are able to understand words such as "no," "shoe," and "juice," family members' names, and other words like "hello" and "bye-bye."

Some research shows that girls lead boys in their understanding of words; others show that the sexes do not differ. But all studies find a tremendous range: at nine months, some babies understand just eleven words, whereas others comprehend as many as 154. By sixteen months, the gap widens, with the bottom 10 percent of children understanding just 92 words and the top 10 percent understanding 321 words.

These studies highlight how much difference a little stimulation can make when neural connections in a baby's brain are wiring up. Extra one-on-one repetition, conversing and singing can make a startling difference to your son's language abilities.

Boosting a boy's early pre-language abilities

Studies show that, particularly during the first six months, daily massage and warm, loving touch accelerates brain development. It is especially beneficial to boys, whose sense of touch is not as highly developed at birth as it is in girls.

One of the best ways to stimulate your baby's brain is to have "conversations" together. Copy your baby's actions and movements, comment on them, speaking with lots of intonation, not too quickly and louder than you normally would. This is especially important between the ages of four and eight months.

Reading and sharing books as early as six months is especially good for boys, as it accelerates left-hemisphere development. Talk about the pictures, make strange noises and encourage your child to copy your sound effects and help you find various pictures.

Boys' visual and verbal memory abilities tend to lag behind those of girls because of slower left-hemisphere development. As he gets older, encourage your son's development by combining words with memorable sensory experiences.

○ Talk about the soft fur of a puppy or other animal and let him feel it.

○ Talk about the icy cold of ice cream and let him taste it.

○ Describe the different appearance of objects and people and let him touch or smell them.

○ Tell him about different sounds or music as he hears them.

○ Recount events together and act them out.

○ Teach your son action songs and rhymes.

2 First words

A child's first birthday is a wonderful and special occasion. And it's around this time that your child's true language begins. Most babies say their first word within a month or two of reaching birthday number one. Interestingly, the delay between understanding words and being able to *say* them parallels exactly what's happening in the brain. The growth of the synapses (or connections) in the brain region in charge of *learning* words reaches a peak from eight to twenty months. Synaptic growth in the region in charge of *speaking* words, on the other hand, does not reach a peak until between fifteen months and two years.

Is it true that girls begin speaking before boys?

A strong female advantage for verbal abilities, attributed to hormones and biology, has been taken for granted for many years. In a 1987 study involving over 9,000 children, girls were found to score more highly on a number of verbal tests. However, a year later, a comprehensive analysis of 165 language studies, representing almost 1.5 million subjects, found that differences were very small. Other studies show that, even if differences do exist, boys catch up by the age of four, and many studies reveal no differences between boys and girls at all. In a large American study, based in San Diego in 1994 involving over 1,800 children, language abilities were found to differ ever so slightly in favor of girls. But the differences were so small that if you were to compare the abilities of 100 pairs of same-age boys and girls, usually on only one occasion would the language abilities of the girl be better than those of the boy.

Not unlike the studies investigating children's receptive vocabularies (words they understand but cannot say), the most striking aspect of these studies is the vast range in abilities between individual children of the same age, irrespective of sex.

Did you know...?

There are many boys who excel in verbal skills, and many girls who are slow to begin talking. Boys, however, do appear less robust than girls when it comes to speech problems. Although stuttering, for instance, affects only 1 percent of all children under the age of twelve, boys who stutter outnumber girls by about three to one.

The role of biology

Research findings about the sex differences in brain structure and sequence of brain development help to explain why females score more highly on verbal fluency tests, whereas on other verbal tests, such as vocabulary size and verbal reasoning, the sexes perform indistinguishably from each other.

The "tasty toys" experiment (see page 39) helps to illustrate that, although boys' and girls' brains use the same amount of energy in building neural networks and synaptic connections in the early years, their choice of building site at any given time is likely to differ. If girls are ahead of boys in developing language skills, it is because boys are developing spatial skills in advance of girls; these timing differences in building sites are likely to account for perceived differences.

Recent research in the neurosciences indicates that boys' poorer literacy performance at school has less to do with biology and more to do with how reading is currently being taught (see Chapter 6).

Differing patterns of neural growth

Vision Boys make less eye contact with their mothers than girls do and are interested in global space more than immediate space.
Result Girls may spend more time, earlier on than boys, focusing on their mother's lips and paying attention to speech.

Motor skills At birth, boys are more wakeful and move their limbs more than girls. They develop gross motor skills before fine motor skills.
Result Greater activity levels of boys, as they practice these skills, could lead to more time spent exploring away from the parent's side and to fewer conversational interactions.

Family differences

What is striking is that socio-economic class makes far more difference than gender does in determining a child's language abilities.

In a remarkable study in the United States, children's language development was followed from the age of nine months to three years. The children's families were classified as "professional," "middle class," or "on welfare." At the end of this time, the researchers found that differences in the kinds of parent-child interactions observed in these families had added up to produce some alarming differences in the children's language abilities. Children from the first

Language milestones

The range in children's developing language abilities is so vast, it is difficult to think in terms of the "average child." These ranges (gleaned from a number of studies) represent the time period when most children achieve these milestones. But, even if your son's progress falls outside these ranges, keep in mind that his progress is still likely to be within the range of what is considered normal for his age.

ACTIVITY	BOYS	GIRLS
Baby responds to the word "no"; attends to other sounds in the environment besides speech	4–6 months	4–6 months
Babbling begins	4–6 months	4–6 months
Baby obviously listens to you; enjoys finger-play, recognizes the names of familiar people and things	9–14 months	8–13 months
Understands about 70 words	12+ months	12+ months
Begins to produce spoken words or approximations	11–14 months	10–13 months
Is able to say 50 words	17–23 months	15–21 months
Combines two words	18–22 months	16–20 months
Can identify five body parts	23–25 months	22–24 months
Can say 200–300 words; understands 400+ words	from 32 months	from 30 months
Says three-word sentences	from 30 months	from 28 months
Speech is 90–100 percent intelligible	from 3 to 4 years	from 3 to 4 years

group had an average spoken vocabulary of 1,115 words, from the second group 750 words, and from the third group just 525 words.

Late talkers

Although all children learn language in a very predictable pattern – babbling, single words, two- and three-word phrases, grammar and syntax – because there is such wide variation at the early stages, parents can't help but make comparisons. They worry.

Parents of boys may worry more often. Among the 3 to 4 percent of children with speech delays, about 60 percent are boys. There are two factors that might contribute to this sex bias. First, the most common cause of language delays is chronic ear infections, which are more common among boys than girls. Second, twin studies suggest that there may be a genetic component to speech delays, once again putting boys more at risk (see Chapter 4).

However, because children vary so widely in their language development, speech delay is difficult to diagnose. In general, by two years of age, your son should be speaking in three-word sentences – "Me do it!" – and about three-quarters of what he says should be intelligible. If, however, you have any doubts about your son's language development before that, have his hearing checked by your family doctor. If you prefer to seek specialist help right away then ask friends or family if they can recommend an audiologist; and then, if necessary, have his neurological development assessed by a neurologist.

Most late talkers, though, are found to be otherwise completely normal. So what happens to them? A great deal of evidence shows that language-delayed, but otherwise normal, children catch up completely. Any intellectual or academic repercussions are usually minor. Fortunately, provided that there are no major underlying problems, the development of language appears to be fairly resilient, at least for the first six or seven years of life.

Late-talking boys: budding Einsteins?

Misdiagnosis in children who talk late is not uncommon. According to one neuroscientist, three-quarters of the medical histories she sees contain at least one report that is "completely off the mark." Her research revealed the following patterns in late-talking children.

○ The average age talking began was four.

○ The majority were boys.

○ As toddlers, most had displayed an unusual ability to do puzzles.

○ Most displayed remarkable memories.

○ Many were musically or mathematically inclined, or both.

○ Most had more than one close relative who played a musical instrument.

Recently, in a brain-scanning study in Miami, it was found that when speech-delayed children heard recordings of their mother's speech, activity in their brains was primarily confined to the right hemisphere; 86 percent were right-dominant (compared with 44 percent of "'normal speech" children being right-dominant). Might these findings be linked to the fact that, like Einstein (who was also a late talker), many gifted boys have unusual right-hemisphere skills?

2 Exposure to language

We now know that the process of learning alters brain structure. Is it possible that experience, in the form of lots of verbal interaction, could overcome any biological factors that may operate to slow down or delay boys' language development? And do parents talk to boys and girls in equal amounts?

Both girls and boys are exposed to language from birth, but are they exposed to the same amount? It is easy to assume that parents talk to their sons and daughters for the same amounts of time – but *do* they?

Researchers have painstakingly investigated this issue. Some evidence shows that parents are egalitarian; they talk to sons and daughters for the same amount of time, regardless of sex. Other research puts a wrinkle in these findings. Instead, it seems that mothers and fathers may behave differently. Mothers initiate "conversations" or verbal play for equivalent amounts of time with sons or with daughters. Fathers, on the other hand, may not be so even-handed. One study showed that they talk more with their daughters than with their sons.

Measuring verbal interaction

However, when we delve deeper, we find a new wrinkle. A third study measured the amount of time different kinds of interactions between mother and baby occurred during free play. The researchers observed parents and children on three occasions: at four months, eight months and twelve months. The amount of time mothers spent verbally encouraging their daughters did not differ at any of these times.

But, to their surprise, something unexpected occurred with mothers and sons. When boy babies were four months and twelve months old, the amount of verbal encouragement their mothers gave them was similar to the mothers of girls. At eight months, however, the researchers discovered that the extent to which mothers of boys engaged in verbal interactions had decreased significantly since they were first observed when the babies were four months old. This seemed to indicate that boys, as compared with girls, are exposed to less language in their first year.

Crucial timing

The first two years of a child's life are critical for language development, and if a child does not learn a language by the age of six, evidence (from "wild" children and brain injury studies) indicates that it is unlikely he or she ever will. A period of four or five months during the first year of life in which boys hear less language than girls do could make a difference in the age at which they begin talking.

By eight months, babies are beginning to crawl, and the researchers noted that the boy babies were more active and exploratory than the girls and tended to elicit behavior from their mothers that encouraged motor development, often at the expense of language stimulation. It may be important for parents of boys, then, to consciously maintain their verbal interactions with their sons around this time.

Q How early should I try to encourage my son's verbal abilities?

A An intriguing study showed that a special program of language stimulation (see page 49) begun at three months of age gave babies of both sexes a surprising lead over babies who did not begin the program until six or eight months of age. Basically, one of the easiest ways to boost your son's language ability is to have fun talking with him *a lot*, and *from birth*.

Q My son is sixteen months old but can say only five or six words. Should I be worried?

A There is no need to worry. The growth of spoken words is very slow to begin with. Although some children can say 50 words by thirteen months, others may take 25 months to reach this stage. Once your son can say 50 words, things will speed up. Nearly all children take just two months to progress from 50 to 100 words.

2 Secrets of superior language experience

Some children grow up being exposed to an abundance of conversation from parents, siblings, relatives and friends, whereas others are raised in quieter, less-talkative households. How does the home environment affect your son's speech development? And what is the ideal environment for maximizing his verbal potential?

After years of conjecture, psychologists do, at last, have a fairly clear idea about the factors that count. The bulk of this information comes from an intensive, cleverly conceived study of language development conducted by Betty Hart and Todd Risley. Researchers visited 40 Kansas families every month during the first three years of their children's lives to make detailed observations of parents' ways of interacting with their children. They kept track of children's vocabulary size and the rate of language growth, and finally, when the children reached the age of three, the researchers measured their verbal intelligence quotients (IQs).

Quantity of language

The first thing that stood out was that the sheer *amount* of talk addressed directly to a child makes a dramatic difference. Some children heard an average of 600 words an hour spoken to them, whereas others heard twice as many, more than 1,200 words an hour. This was a startling difference. Would it make any difference to children's language learning?

When the researchers looked at the connection between words heard and the children's language progress, it was clear that the children whose parents spoke to or responded to them more over this early period in their lives had larger, faster-growing vocabularies as well as significantly higher verbal IQ scores than those children whose parents spoke fewer words to them.

So, the more words children hear, the larger their vocabulary will be and the faster it will continue to grow. However, it is crucially important to remember this means the number of words addressed directly to the child. Children who overhear a lot of telephone conversations, other people conversing or dialogue on television will not develop language skills as they should. Deaf parents were once advised to expose their hearing babies to speech on television, but the babies did not learn how to speak.

What a difference a word makes...

As boys' language development is more vulnerable to genetic or environmental influences compared with that of girls, you may like to try some of the activities outlined here, developed by an educational psychologist, Dr. William Fowler. In a study using his methods parents were trained to stimulate their child's language progress by anticipating and encouraging development *before* it happened. They did this by

- ○ making syllable sounds for their babies before they were babbling,
- ○ labeling objects as soon as their babies were attracted to them,
- ○ encouraging longer utterances when the babies were only beginning to say single words,
- ○ engaging in "theme" play.

The results were striking. Stimulated children (both girls and boys)

- ○ spoke their first words between seven and nine months,
- ○ began combining words by the time they were a year old,
- ○ spoke in sentences as early as ten months,
- ○ had mastered grammar rules by the age of two (a milestone normally achieved at four),
- ○ had nearly all learned to read before starting school,
- ○ were more likely (62 percent) to be placed in a gifted or accelerated class in senior school.

How to increase the *quantity* of words your son hears

Although the following strategies will enhance language development for both sexes, they are particularly important to boys, who are more vulnerable to ear infections (see page 80) and testosterone-influenced development of the right hemisphere of the brain.

- ○ From an early age, give names or labels to any objects, actions or people that attract your son's interest and attention.

- ○ Use a variety of adjectives (big, soft, cold), adverbs (fast, slowly, quickly, loudly), prepositions (in, out, behind) and pronouns (you, me, he, his), rather than just nouns and verbs.

- ○ Use lots of repetition, repeating favorite rhymes, action songs and finger-plays.

- ○ Make substitutions: the red (blue/tiny/bouncy/plastic/squeaky) ball.

- ○ Expand on your son's words (that car/that little car/that little red car/that little red car is zooming away!).

- ○ Ask "wh-" questions (who? what? where? when? why?).

- ○ Discuss and recall events with your son, so he gets used to describing his day.

2 Quality of language counts, too

Continuing on in the landmark Hart and Risley study (see page 48), researchers were able to determine that it is not simply the quantity of language that matters – *the way in which parents spoke to their children* profoundly affected the children's language learning as well. When children from the study were followed up six years later, those whose parents spoke to them most, and in certain ways, continued to excel at language skills, including reading, spelling, speaking, and listening abilities.

Essentially, the study revealed that two factors really counted: parents' vocabulary and parents' approach or tone. Children whose parents used a greater variety of words and sentences turned out to have superior language skills and IQ scores. In terms of tone, three factors made a difference:

○ how often parents responded positively (with praise) rather than negatively (with criticism) to their child's actions or words.

○ the degree to which parents invited their children to do things rather than issued imperatives ("Don't!" "Stop it!" "I said no!"). (Although this research did not look at sex differences, other research indicates that boys tend to attract more direct orders from their parents than girls do.)

○ how attentive and responsive parents were toward their child (affirming or repeating their child's words, following their child's words with questions and discussion).

Some mothers were consistently positive toward their children but others were seven times more likely to respond negatively. Some moms were highly responsive and issued few direct orders; others made negative or prohibitive remarks 80 percent of the time.

A wide range of parenting styles was seen but, disturbingly, these differences in conversational approach turned out to be linked to social class. Does this mean that socio-economic background seals a child's fate in the language learning stakes?

Not entirely. The researchers found that the way parents interact with their children is actually far more important than social class. Within each class, there are parents who talk more, use a greater variety of words and sentences, who ask more often than tell their children what to do, and who consistently respond in positive rather than negative ways to their children's speech and behavior. These are the parents who are going to raise more verbally able children, whatever their sex, level of education or economic background.

Language: the key to intelligence?

Language abilities are related to full-scale IQ scores since vocabulary scores are strongly related to reading comprehension. The development of language opens the door to almost unlimited learning. Although half our language abilities depend on our genes, only very small environmental differences can lead to staggering differences in a child's intellectual potential.

Hot tips for accelerating early language learning

○ Speak clearly and enunciate your words slowly. Talk to your child at a level appropriate to his age. Relate new words to concepts that your child already understands.

○ Take turns with your son. Give your child the chance to respond to you – either vocally or through gestures or movements.

○ Have lots of face-to-face conversations so that your child can see how you move your lips as you say the words.

○ Repeat your child's first attempts to speak. Baby boys, in particular, simply love the sense of control they feel when you imitate them.

○ Your child's first words are likely to be mispronounced. You will need to listen extremely carefully in order to avoid missing them. If you catch them and respond, your child's language development will receive an enormous boost.

○ Don't correct grammar. This is particularly discouraging to boys' egos, giving them the message, "I'm pretty useless at this talking business." Ignore mistakes, but provide a good example with your own speech.

○ For boys, songs are especially beneficial. Songs combine words (left hemisphere) and melody (right hemisphere). Singing songs together will speed the comprehensive growth of neural connections in your son's brain. If you include movement or dancing as well, it will harness some of those high activity levels.

○ Make learning fun. Play word games, and recite nursery rhymes and action songs (buy some tapes or CDs if you need ideas).

○ Read to your child every day, making it an opportunity to cuddle (boys have an even greater need than girls for cuddling; see page 142) and have some fun. Use books as a starting point for conversation. Children who have stories read to them early and often have better language skills and vocabulary many years later than those who miss out on this activity.

○ Although the first six or seven years of a child's life are a critical period for language, this period declines only gradually. Children of all ages can benefit from increased language stimulation – less television, more conversation and reading. Research shows that the more years of high school and university a person completes, the longer the neural pathways in the word-learning and language regions of their brains.

3 emotional life

3 Nature or nurture?

Fran and Stephen's baby Jack is only six months old, but from the start his behavior has been unlike his sister's. For one thing, he sleeps lightly and when awake he almost constantly waves his arms and legs around. He also appears to engage people in less eye contact, preferring instead to gaze at nearby objects. His parents wonder whether Jack's ways are simply due to his personality or *because he is a boy*. They feel sure that they have acted no differently toward him than toward his sister; but their friends have made similar observations about their little boys, so they can only conclude that these observed gender differences are largely innate.

So, do scientific studies support this parental observation and show that boys and girls differ simply because of their genes? Well, in short, yes, they do! A growing body of research shows that there really *are* some behavioral differences between baby boys and baby girls that appear to be built in. As early as the first day of life, for instance, girl babies establish and maintain eye contact more than boy babies do. They orientate to faces and voices more frequently, on average, than their male equivalents do, and by six months of age, baby girls demonstrate a better memory for familiar faces. These characteristics are related to sex differences in vision development, as we saw in Chapter 2.

Reactions to others' feelings

Other research studies, however, provide more clear evidence that the sexes differ both socially and emotionally. Such research shows that while baby girls react with greater empathy to the distress of others, boys appear to be more disturbed by it. Baby girls are found to cry longer than boys when they are exposed to the cry of another infant, whereas in baby boys there is a noticeable physical reaction – their heart rates increase dramatically. Additionally, most experiments find that baby boys are more physically active both when they are asleep and when they are awake.

However, these differences, where they do exist, are very small. There will also be boy babies who sleep longer and more soundly than their sisters did, and who are equally attracted to the voices and faces around them. Moreover, after years of debate, scientists now generally agree that gender-specific behavior is not due to nature alone, but represents a complex blend of both nature and nurture.

Subconscious parental influences

Adults treat boys and girls differently in many ways that they may not even be aware of. Even the smallest biological differences in early infant behavior elicit different responses from their parents. So, it seems impossible to avoid: inevitably boys and girls end up being treated differently.

These differences can be quite subtle and subconscious. For instance, mothers smile more at their daughters than at their sons, perhaps simply because their daughters are more responsive to them. (In Chapter 2 we saw that there is a period during the first year when mothers talk more to their daughters than their sons, maybe because daughters are more inclined to stay close or, again, are more responsive.)

Fathers, meanwhile, engage their sons far more than their daughters in rough, gently aggressive, physical play. But, this may simply be because boys, physically stronger and bigger than girls, seem to enjoy wrestling with their dads more. So, parents treat boys and girls differently simply because

they *are* different to start with. But other factors are also at play. Parents may interact with their sons and daughters in different ways because culture has trained them to have distinct sets of expectations for each sex. Society stereotypes girls as the more verbal, emotive sex. Do parents talk to girls more as a result? Are they more understanding and compassionate toward a daughter's emotional displays? Boys are expected to be brave and daring, and not to cry. And, to what extent might parents encourage their son's physical prowess at the expense of encouraging his language and emotional development?

In recent years, non-invasive methods of brain-scanning mean that scientists are discovering some differences in the way the brains of males and females develop with respect to their social and emotional systems. These findings may help us, as parents, to understand why our children behave as they do.

3 The emotional quotient

Let's imagine a situation where you have two sons. The first boy excels at mathematics, but he likes to work on his own, is socially inept and has few, if any, friends. This son has a very high intelligence quotient or IQ. The second child works hard to obtain the same level of achievement as his brother (although he might not attain it) but has a sunny disposition and gets along brilliantly with other people. This son has what we call a high emotional quotient or EQ. Which son do you think has the better chance of finding success and happiness?

Undoubtedly, you will choose the second son. This is because you know that to get ahead in today's world, you must be prepared to work hard and you must be a pleasure to work hard with! Emotional intelligence – the ability to recognize and control one's own feelings, as well as to read and respond to the feelings of others – is likely to play a greater part in your son's future success than his intellectual abilities.

What is EQ?

A Yale psychologist, Peter Salovey, identifies five types of emotional intelligence:

○ **Emotional attunement** – the ability to recognize one's own feelings, awareness of how it feels to be happy, sad, frustrated, angry or bored.

○ **Emotional management** – the ability to keep emotions in check, to behave in ways that are considered appropriate, to cheer oneself up after a big setback or to rein in a temper tantrum mid-stream.

○ **Self-motivation** – the ability to delay gratification (see the "marshmallow test," opposite).

○ **Empathy** – the ability to "read" others' feelings, to understand that a certain tone of voice or facial expression carries with it a specific meaning.

○ **Relationship management** – the ability to form relationships with other people easily while maintaining independence and to know how to defuse difficult situations.

It may be more difficult for boys than girls to progress in these areas (as we shall see), but the better your son becomes at these emotional intelligence skills, the more certain his future success.

The "marshmallow test"

In this Stanford University experiment no differences were found between four-year-old boys and girls in the ability to delay gratification. Each child was given a marshmallow and told that they could eat it now, in which case they would get only the one marshmallow, or they could wait until the experimenter returned in fifteen minutes, in which case they would get a second marshmallow and could then eat them both.

Some children stuffed the marshmallow in their mouth as soon as the experimenter left the room. Others, though, fiddled and squirmed, talked or sang songs to themselves, some even covered their eyes to prevent themselves from seeing the marshmallow, but somehow all these children managed to hold out for the greater reward of two marshmallows.

Astonishingly, the children's performance on this test was found to predict their success at the end of high school better than their age four IQ scores! Those children able to control themselves had – twelve to fourteen years later – higher grades and better test scores and were more self-reliant and socially competent than their less restrained peers.

Boys' early social-emotional development

The parts of the brain that control feelings develop, like most of the brain, from the bottom to the top. Newborn babies are in possession of only about half their emotional hardware. This means that, although they react to painful, pleasurable or surprising stimuli, they have no upper brain awareness of *how* they feel in the same way that an older child does.

During the second six months, however, the higher brain regions in the front of the brain and behind the eyes gradually assume more and more control over the lower, more instinctual regions. This is when babies really begin to *feel* the emotions that their faces show. It's also when babies become genuine artistes at being able to communicate exactly what they feel and want.

It is about this time that babies begin to show real affection toward those they know well and along with this an increasing awareness that others are strangers. This important attachment/stranger anxiety milestone reflects what's going on in the brain. It shows not only the development of the higher, thinking part of the emotional system but also the development within this region of the center for short-term memory. This is the beginning of *object permanence* –

the realization that things or people continue to exist even though you can't see them. Until this region develops, it's difficult for a baby to become attached to someone who they cannot remember exists.

The neural systems in the upper emotional centers of the brain, which help in controlling impulses, take a notoriously long time to mature, and evidence suggests this takes even longer in boys. On average, synapses reach a maximum density in this region by the age of seven. A period of pruning follows before more neural growth begins during adolescence. For males, the whole process is not complete until their late twenties.

3 The value of SPEED

It's great to feel that what you do makes such a difference in the kind of grown-up your child will become. You can make the most of your son's social, emotional and, in turn, intellectual potential by providing a healthy, safe, loving, attentive, emotionally balanced and predictable home environment. The following six factors are known to affect all children's social and emotional growth, but they prove even more crucial to boys' experiences than to girls'.

1 The need to feel safe

From the beginning of his or her life, a baby needs to feel safe. When a baby's bodily needs (food, warmth and so on) are attended to promptly, the brain can begin to grow properly. In one recent brain-scanning experiment, the brains of severely neglected children were compared with those of children from loving homes and were found to be 30 percent smaller than those of normal children.

When a baby's basic survival needs are not met, the lower, more primitive neural pathways in the brain are repeatedly activated, and as a result, little energy can be devoted to the development of other, higher structures within the brain.

Although a recent survey revealed that 44 percent of parents and 60 percent of grandparents believe that picking up a three-month-old baby every time he cries will spoil the child, babies cannot be spoiled. If babies are not picked up when they cry (and it's important to keep in mind that boy babies may be more demanding and fractious than girls), their levels of stress and distress may build up and slow the rate at which they are able to learn.

2 The need to feel special

Babies need physical affection, love and attention. Some research shows that when deprived of affection, boys' development suffers more than girls'. In a study examining children's impulse control and ability to delay gratification it was found that the

---

SPEED

A child needs

○ **S**afety and to know he is special.

○ **P**redictability.

○ **E**qual amounts of freedom and limits.

○ **E**xperiences that are diverse.

○ **D**iscipline.

quality of a mother's emotional bond with her child at the age of two predicted how well her *son*, but *not her daughter*, was able to perform a test such as the "marshmallow test" (see page 57) at the age of six. Probably the most important contribution any parent can make to a child's future success and happiness is to ensure that they feel truly loved and admired for all their own special qualities.

The mother represents the first socio-emotional interaction the child experiences and lays the foundation for all of a child's later behavior. Breast-feeding helps to create the sort of close physical and emotional bond that is needed. Some evidence suggests that babies, and especially boys, who are breast-fed for longer (more than one year) are not only more advanced than others intellectually, but better adjusted socially and emotionally as well.

Studies show that the earlier babies form close, loving relationships the better in terms of their overall brain development. Researchers assessing six-year-olds who had been adopted from Romanian orphanages found that, of those adopted before the age of six months, 69 percent were functioning "normally," whereas of those adopted between the ages of seven months and two years of age, the proportion dropped to 43 percent. Of the children adopted between the ages of two and three and a half years, only 22 percent were functionally normally.

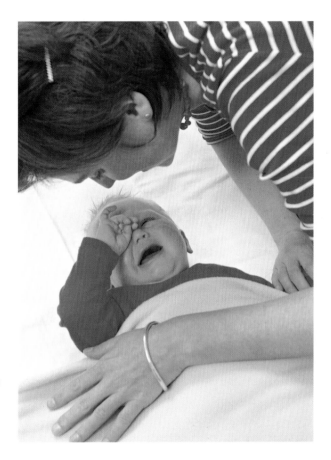

3 The need for predictability

A child needs to feel confident about what to expect from people. Babies raised in violent homes or by parents who are indifferent to them or who suffer from mental illness experience damaging amounts of stress. Stress hormones affect these babies' brains, more so for boys (who tend to be more anxious than girls), altering how their brains develop.

In one study, one-year-old babies with high stress hormone levels showed abnormally low levels of electrical activity in certain parts of the emotional systems of their brains. Their lower brain circuits (that handled anxiety and fear) were always activated, while higher brain regions (involved in complex thought and empathy) were not activated and did not develop. In unpredictable settings, children do not develop the ability to understand how others feel since all their brain's resources have been concentrated on dealing with the fear engendered by the uncertainty in their life. They are, quite literally, emotionally retarded.

Babies securely attached to their mothers, however, show significantly less release of stress hormones than those who are not securely attached, even in the face of strange or fearful events. And it's not just mothers who can protect their children's brains from the damaging effects of stress. Studies with unfamiliar babysitters, for example, have shown that as long as the caregiver is friendly, playful and sensitive, babies will not experience significant stress.

Q Is it normal for my five-year-old son to want nothing to do with girls?

A Children start segregating by sex at around two and a half. By the age of four, playing with same-sex peers occurs three times more often. Among six-year-olds, segregation occurs eleven times more often. Girls pull away before boys, but by the age of five or six, boys more adamantly prefer to play with their own sex, rating girls as "wimpy" and uninteresting.

Q Are young girls interested in social relationships earlier than boys?

A A study examining pre-schoolers' amount of "emotion talk" found that two-year-old girls talked much more about their own and other people's feelings than their male equivalents did. As boys grew older they gradually referred to emotions more frequently.

4 The need for equal amounts of freedom and limits

To achieve their social and emotional potential and to learn how to delay gratification, children need to experience a balance of freedom and limits. This involves setting clear rules and responding consistently when they are broken. Boys like to see how far they can push the limits, and when you respond consistently your son will gain a sense that you care about his learning. On the other hand, do not make rules that are too difficult for your son to comply with. Parents of children, especially boys, with chronic discipline problems often have unrealistic expectations and are overly controlling. Allowing a certain amount of freedom is an excellent boost to self-confidence.

5 The need for enriching experiences

Evidence shows that children who are exposed to intellectually stimulating experiences at the age of two can better control their feelings and delay gratification at six. Children also benefit from experiencing a variety of emotions and different social relationships. Encouraging boys to talk about their feelings boosts their EQ (see page 56); it helps them learn ways to handle their emotions, and understand and empathize with others. The opportunity to form relationships with both parents (if possible), relatives, children of the same age and with groups of people gives a child the chance to develop and practice social skills.

6 The need for discipline

Boys and girls both need to experience some discipline in order to thrive, but they may need different forms. In an illuminating experiment with one-year-olds, boys and girls behaved differently when a physical barrier was placed between them and something that they wanted. The little boys tended to spend their time trying to knock down the barrier, whereas the girls spent a lot of their time seeking help from their mothers.

These findings support those from other experiments in which children of the same sex are observed as they play together in an unstructured setting. Boys engage in higher energy, less verbal activities and show less compliance than girls. Discipline needs to be tailored accordingly. Parents may need to apply firmer discipline with boys, and verbal instructions may be less effective than taking certain types of action (see page 71).

Developing gender identity

A strong influence on behavior comes from the gender children identify with. But parents who do not push their children too strongly into gender-typical behavior give their children a chance to develop their own unique talents, whatever they may be.

Television and other influences, though, teach children to tell the difference between the sexes very early. So far, apart from the study on three-month-olds mentioned in Chapter 1 (see page 18), evidence suggests that girls and boys reach gender-identity milestones at the same average ages (see box below).

AT	CHILDREN CAN...
6 months	tell men from women seen head to toe.
10 months	tell men from women by face alone.
2–2½ years	label pictures of boys and girls correctly.
2–3 years	identify their own gender (by placing a picture of themselves in the correct gender group).

How boys' brains shape their behavior

A child's emotional and social behavior are stimulated and regulated through a network that extends through several brain regions, from the primitive areas deep within the brain to the more sophisticated regions in the frontal brain. This system is known as the *limbic* system.

In the lower regions deep within the brain are the emotion-arousal center called the amygdala (the "tiger [T] in boys' tanks") and the hypothalamus (H), the hormone-triggering region that induces physical responses in the face of emotional arousal or stress (see illustration below). Activity in these lower regions triggers responses upward and forward into a frontal region (F) behind the eyes and forehead (governing social responses, control of emotions, executive control of actions) and into a region deep under the temples, a memory-making region (M) that helps the brain decide whether responses to fear or anxiety should be turned on in other parts of the brain.

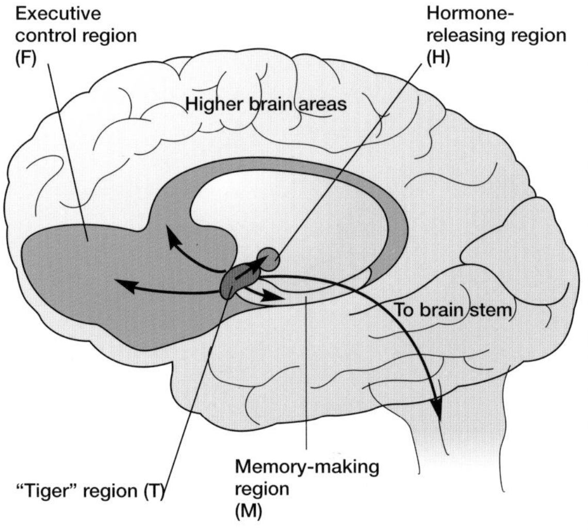

By measuring the electrical activity in children's brains, neuroscientists now know that boys and girls develop these regions at different rates. From two months to six years of age, boys' brains show greater activity and growth in a part of region F that is involved with planning and practicality of gross motor movements; girls, meanwhile, show greater neural growth and activity in a different part of F as well as in region M. After the age of six, these patterns of growth shift and boys' and girls' brains begin to focus on the development of new regions.

Psychologists' tests have confirmed these neurological differences. Knowing what happens in terms of brain growth, one would predict that young girls should outperform boys in visual matching tests that rely on memory (M), whereas boys are expected to perform better in object reversal tests, which depend on the divergent thinking parts of region F. And, with children aged one to four and a half, this is exactly the case. "Object reversal" tests measure how quickly

Structures in the brain's social-emotional system

Executive control region (F)

Hormone-releasing region (H)

Higher brain areas

To brain stem

"Tiger" region (T)

Memory-making region (M)

Did you know...?

A study found that boys' right hemispheres are more accurate at correctly identifying facial emotions than their left, while the opposite is true for girls. The boys' right-hemisphere approach is a more global one, but the girls' left-hemisphere approach, focusing on the finer detail, may explain why girls tend to be better than boys at reading the emotions on people's faces.

children can learn that choosing the smaller of two objects elicits a reward when previously, choosing the larger one produced the reward. Although the tests relate more to memory than emotional development, they do confirm that two of the brain regions known to underlie social-emotional experience develop at different rates in the two sexes.

Similarly, other neural networks governing social development develop differently for boys and girls. Girls' brains make it a priority to grow strong links between regions in the front (that control decisions about propriety, practicality and social conventions) and the memory-making region. Boys' brains focus instead on the development of neural connections between parts of the F region and the visual area, at the back of the brain. Suddenly, it begins to make sense why young boys are superior to girls in their visual targeting and visual tracking abilities (and enjoy throwing things!)

and why girls, from a very early age, appear to be more fascinated with social interactions. These different abilities will also affect the way they interact with others and develop socially.

3 Individual temperaments

So far in this book we have looked at and discussed some of the small ways in which boys and girls differ in their behavior, and how these differences are often evident from birth. But all children differ socially and emotionally, regardless of their sex. One child may be impulsive, whereas the other is more cautious. One is a good sleeper and easily pacified, the other is restless, fidgety and hard to console. Is there something about the architecture of their brains that determines these differences? Or is it caused by something else?

Unfortunately, despite some of the great strides made in neurobiology in recent years, very little is known about the neural basis of innate temperamental differences. However, there is one area of human temperament that neuroscientists do know something about: the tendency to be shy or bold.

Is your son shy or bold?

Many toddlers are initially shy in a new environment, but some children – about 15 percent of all toddlers, both male and female – never seem to relax, no matter how friendly the new people are or how enticing they find the new toys. At the other end of the spectrum are another 15 percent of toddlers who are decidedly uninhibited.

Twin studies show that shyness or boldness is inherited; these traits are largely owing to our genes. And a study of children aged between four and a half and seven years of age revealed no sex differences in the incidence of reticent behavior.

Research shows, as well, that the tendency to withdraw or approach in the face of novelty is one of the more stable of emotional traits. But, demonstrating the fact that environment can play a substantial role, some toddlers (about 40 percent) do manage to grow out of their extreme shyness by the time it's time for them to enter pre-school.

Cultural expectations, however, may also play a role here. Society generally regards shyness as a more acceptable trait in a girl than in a boy, and different cultures encourage or inhibit boldness in their children.

When it comes to uninhibited behavior, however, environmental influences may not have as great an effect (but see page 67). Children who are uninhibited as toddlers are much more likely to remain that way. Only about 10 percent of children who were bold as toddlers end up becoming more reserved by the time they reach pre-school age.

Feeling uplifted? It's *left* brain. Feeling rotten? It's *right* brain.

Emotions related to fear, distress and anxiety, which produce shy and withdrawn behavior, generally involve higher levels of electrical activity in the *right* frontal area of the brain. In contrast, feelings of joy, interest and affection result in more brain activity in the *left* frontal region.

Four-year-olds who seem happy and readily play and talk with their friends show greater activation of the left frontal brain region, whereas those who are very reserved socially, who tend to isolate themselves and look on while others play, show relatively greater activation of the right frontal area.

Q **My three-year-old son is quite unafraid to talk to other people and likes to run away when we're shopping. If I try to hold his hand he just screams and throws himself onto the floor. How should I deal with this type of behavior?**

A First, be prepared to abandon the idea of a quick fix. A slow program is needed in order to get the results you want. Begin a new shopping strategy. Start by taking very short trips to buy only two or three items. Make a list of the items with your child, perhaps by drawing pictures of the things like milk, a box of cereal, bananas. At the supermarket, do not make an issue of holding his hand; instead, make the experience a game by asking him if he can find the three items. You follow, while he helps. At the end of this, you should tell him how good he was and what fun you had. On the next trip, have a longer list and praise him when he finds things. Eventually, your son may want to help with other tasks – unloading, packing, unpacking – and before you know it, shopping will be a more enjoyable experience for both of you.

Shy or bold: how can parents help?

Parents can encourage extremely shy children to assert themselves more; as statistics show, environmental influences can help at least 40 percent of shy children to overcome their reticence. And as for those children who seem to have no inhibitions whatsoever, research shows that environmental factors may not be completely overruled by biology.

Recent research shows that among children and adolescents ranging in age from six to eighteen years, testosterone levels are not related to risk-taking behavior (part of the uninhibited end of the spectrum) or to depression (part of the inhibited end of the spectrum). What researchers did find, though, was that as the quality of the parent–child relationship increases, risk-taking and depression are much less in evidence. So those six vital SPEED factors described on pages 58–59 are important in balancing your son's inhibitions or lack of them.

Shy boy or wild child?

In terms of your son's future, is it better that he is more at one end of the spectrum than the other? Strangely, a highly inhibited temperament is not a deterrent to a bright future. Possibly

because many inhibited children fear failure more than the uninhibited, if the opportunities are there, many go on to be very successful academically, as well as in their careers and family life. In a British study following the lives of over 12,000

people over a period of 30 years, researchers were surprised to discover that those people who as children often worried, frequently played on their own, cried a lot and were fearful and fussy had a tendency to develop into successful adults. And, what might seem to some parents of boys as an added bonus, a shy, inhibited boy may be less inclined than his peers to become involved in dangerous or risky activities (uninhibited behavior), something teenage boys are more prone to than teenage girls.

But, what about the highly uninhibited? Such children do enjoy particular advantages. They learn a great deal through assertive exploration and their curiosity and confidence in novel social situations. But these children can run into problems. Highly uninhibited boys may become overly aggressive if they do not find adequate positive channels to direct their enthusiasms toward.

Q I have just enrolled my son in pre-school, but he shows no interest in exploring the toys on display or joining in with the  other children. Despite attempts made by the teacher and other children to include him, he remains clinging anxiously to my leg. If I try to leave, he cries and makes a huge fuss. What should I do?

A Don't be discouraged. With persistence, you can coax your son to be more outgoing and actually help to rewire the emotional system in his brain. For a few days, or even weeks, your son may cry every time you try to leave. Don't panic. His tears do not mean that he doesn't like his new school. He may soon grow to love it. He simply doesn't want to be there without you. The first and probably the hardest thing you have to do is leave as calmly as you can. Give your son a big hug, tell him when you'll pick him up (after lunch, nap or whatever) and then depart – even if you hear him wailing behind you. (If you see a meltdown coming, enlist the teacher's help beforehand.)

Teachers say that the most common mistake parents make is to turn back or prolong their good-byes. If you persevere, your son will learn that you are not going to give in. As he learns what to expect, he will actually feel more secure. Although your son may always be a cautious sort, he is likely to have a far happier childhood than if, at this point, you give up and give in.

3 The need to dominate

There are two further areas of human temperament in which scientists are just beginning to discover underlying neurological explanations. These are the tendencies for a child to either want to dominate or want to attack another person. And, in this case, it does seem that gender plays a role.

We have seen that, due to the effects of testosterone, there is one structure in the brain's emotional system that is larger in boys than in girls from a very early age. This is the emotion arousal structure, the "tiger in boys' tanks" (see page 18). Scientists have now been able to demonstrate that this particular gender difference in brain structure is responsible for some interesting differences in boys' and girls' social behavior.

Rough and tumble

Although rough physical play is not an exclusively male activity it occurs much more frequently and more vigorously with boys than with girls. As the "tiger" is in charge of sexual arousal and same-sex competition, we can better understand why boys like to play rough. A number of studies related to this sex difference show that boys spend significantly more of their spare time engaged in competitive group activities such as football and basketball. The evidence is also clear that boys' social play involves larger groups and greater hierarchical organization than girls' play.

Let's play...world domination

Both boys and girls engage in dramatic play, such as having dinner or slaying a dragon, but there is a striking difference in the sort of roles they choose for themselves. Boys playing together tend to take on more varied roles than girls and roles characterized more by fantasy and power (Batman, Superman).

Their play focuses on themes associated with dominance and aggression, such as enacting conflicts between cowboys and Indians. It's as if their "tigers" are driving them to practice handling the emotional aspects of same-sex competition; such an ability will

Doctors and nurses

Four-year-old same-sex boy and girl pairs were secretly videotaped and observed as they played in a room with items suggesting a doctor theme. Although the amount of pretend play did not differ between the boy pairs and the girl pairs, boys argued about who was to be "doctor" 80 percent of the time; girls, in contrast, wanted the doctor role only 33 percent of the time.

Q Can you explain why my four-year-old son has become so bossy?

A From this age, or sometimes even younger, boys are the center of their own universe. They are building a sense of self, trying to work out how much influence they have over others as they assert themselves.

be useful when, for example, they have to cope with sexual jealousy later. So, the male brain predisposes boys to practice social and emotional behaviors that are important for survival and reproduction.

Competitive spirit

Researchers investigating the social motives of seven- to seventeen-year-olds found that, at every age, boys endorsed competitive social behavior more frequently than girls did. A typical boy's view was "I like to do better work than my friends." By contrast, the typical girl said, "I like to learn by working with other students."

A number of studies support these findings. Boys' goals are focused on establishing and maintaining dominance. In one experiment, nine- to twelve-year-olds had to set up rules to distribute money among themselves and their peers. While 75 percent of the boys showed a preference for trying to maximize their own resources compared with others in their group, only 20 percent of girls showed this preference.

Measuring up

Boys' need to establish dominance is related to their fears and worries. Researchers investigated the fears and worries of boys and girls aged four to seven in one study. While girls were found to express worries about family members, boys' main worries concerned their own performance – an illuminating finding and the key to understanding what makes boys tick: *their abiding fear is of not measuring up to their same-sex peers*. It explains why the worst thing that can ever happen to a boy is to be humiliated in front of his friends.

3 Frustration and aggression

Young boys are found to be involved in more aggressive incidents than little girls. Yet, during childhood, testosterone levels between boys and girls do not differ. So, as with the other kinds of behavior seen already, does the key to aggressive behavior lie in the differences in their brains?

Girls' brains concentrate much earlier on developing parts of the frontal system that are involved with censoring social behavior and empathy. By adolescence, they have a significantly larger volume of gray matter in this region, particularly on the left, verbal side of the brain. This also means that girls end up with a very different ratio of frontal-to-arousal gray matter volume from boys, a difference that has important implications for behavior. Girls have more brain tissue used to censor aggressive and angry responses, whereas boys have more brain tissue that initiates aggression and impulsive, angry responses. Violent males do not feel more anger than females but they are less inhibited by fear.

Because of the difference in frontal emotional growth, boys are likely to have fewer connections between this area and the lower arousal center. Consistent with this idea is the recent finding from brain-scans that, in females, brain activity associated with emotions occurs mainly in the higher emotional regions, whereas emotional activity in males is still very concentrated in the lower arousal center.

Q Is the occasional spanking harmful long term?

A Spanking is never a good idea. When an adult hits a child for misbehaving, the message the child receives is that it's OK to hit if you're the big one. Parents are most likely to spank children when they're tired, cross or at their wits' end. If we want our children to put their feelings into words, we need to do the same. Research shows that children who are regularly spanked are naughtier three years down the line than children who receive non-violent forms of discipline.

Q How can I stop my boys' fighting?

A Fighting never fails to get Mom's or Dad's attention. Make sure you don't play this game. Send them to a nearby room; tell them not to come out until they have sorted out their differences – for themselves. Shut the door. This routine will shift their focus.

Bottle up or blow?

It is commonly believed that bottling up anger is unhealthy; venting negative feelings is the healthy thing to do. But a display of anger actually increases feelings of anger, raising testosterone levels in young men. The amygdala is given free rein. If instead, a boy is encouraged to take time out to cool off, he achieves just that. Angry feelings subside; he begins to engage the frontal, inhibitory region of his brain and learns how to control unacceptable behavior.

Tips for temper tantrums

Studies show that parents' discipline styles are strongly related to whether a boy becomes aggressive or violent.

Remain calm Shaking, spanking or shouting at your son will make the tantrum worse.

Distract Focus your son's attention on something else if taking a fascinating, but unsafe, object away from him.

Remove Take your son to a private place to cool down. Stay nearby, but don't try to talk until he is calm.

Ignore An older child may just want attention.

Hold It can be necessary to hold an out-of-control child. Explain you'll hold him until he's calm and so he doesn't hurt anyone. This reassures him and makes him feel safe.

Time out Always insist on a cooling-down period. Later, talk about non-violent ways he could express his feelings.

Comfort Tantrums can be frightening; children may not know why they feel so angry, They need to know that you disapprove only of their behavior, you don't disapprove of *them*. Make sure your son knows you still love him.

Social-emotional gender differences in behavior

DIFFERENCES	REASONS		
	Girls' larger frontal region	Girls' larger frontal-to-arousal region ratio	Fewer connections in boys between higher and lower emotional regions
A study of almost 2,000 children investigated sex differences in impulsiveness, helpfulness and fearfulness over a six-year period (ages five to eleven). At every age, boys were found to be less helpful and more impulsive.	✓	✓	
Ask a girl of six to explain why she is sad and she will be able to tell you. But asking a seventeen-year-old boy to talk about his feelings may be almost as unproductive as asking a six-year-old boy to explain how he feels.		✓	
Girls' social relationships are characterized by greater empathy, more concern for the well-being of other girls, more nurturing, intimacy and social-emotional support than are the relationships that develop among boys.	✓		
Girls aged twelve to sixteen use physical assertion to establish social dominance only a third as frequently as boys.	✓	✓	
A study of pre-schoolers found that boys had almost three times as many fights with each other as girls did.		✓	✓

3 Environmental influences

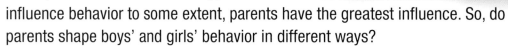

Researchers estimate that nature accounts for around 50 percent of a child's behavior, whereas nurture is responsible for the rest. While peers and cultural stereotypes can influence behavior to some extent, parents have the greatest influence. So, do parents shape boys' and girls' behavior in different ways?

Toy preference: nature or nurture?

Studies show that one area in which parents approach boys and girls differently is in the toy choices they make for them. A huge analysis of the results from 172 studies worldwide that had looked at how parents treat their sons and daughters showed that, for two out of every three boys, parents encouraged gender-typical activities more often than they did with girls.

Parents may also be more influential in more subtle ways: for example in the type of tasks and activities their children see them doing. But research with very young children also appears to show an innate gender bias in the children's choice of toys: boys choosing construction and wheeled toys, and girls opting for dolls and soft toys.

Ways of conversing: nature or nurture?

Evidence from a number of language research studies reveals the following interesting findings:
- ○ Fathers, especially when talking to sons, issue twice as many direct orders as mothers. Because of this, many statements by fathers to boys are very brief.

- ○ Fathers interrupt their children more than mothers do, regardless of the child's sex.
- ○ Both mothers and fathers interrupt girls more often than they do boys.
- ○ As many as 38 percent of fathers' utterances in the home are direct imperatives.
- ○ Fathers' speech at home includes rare vocabulary ("construction site"), threats ("Don't go in there or I'll tan your hide"), and somewhat disparaging nicknames ("little monkey," "tough guy").
- ○ Both parents direct more negative statements and more prohibitions ("Don't touch that") toward boys.

Do children pick up on their parents' way of speaking? In general, evidence suggests that they do:
- ○ By the age of four, boys use more direct imperatives than girls.
- ○ In same-sex pairs, as many as 36 percent of boys' utterances to each other are either direct imperatives or prohibitions, versus 12 percent for girls.
- ○ In a puppet play task, both boys and girls role-playing "fathers" used many imperatives, but when role-playing "mothers" used few.

72 emotional life

○ Boys interrupt girls more than girls interrupt boys in mixed-sex conversations.

○ When five-year-old, same-sex pairs played "doctor," girls used twice as many indirect requests as boys. ("Shall we pretend he cried?" "Could you give me the stethoscope?" "That's your bed, right?" "Now let's cover him up.")

Researchers find it difficult, however, to distinguish cause and effect. Although children clearly do pay attention to how their mothers and fathers talk to each other and to them, the ways boys and girls behave might elicit different reactions from their parents. Boys may attract more direct imperatives because they are more active and assertive than girls.

Interestingly, in the study involving five-year-olds playing "doctor" (conducted by Jacqueline Sachs at the University of Connecticut in 1987), boys often asked what their friend was thinking ("Do you need a shot?" "Are you sick?"), whereas girls often checked out one another's attitudes and feelings ("Does it hurt?").

So, with both nature- and nurture-related sex differences in mind, parents can best accelerate their son's emotional development by encouraging him to tune in to his feelings.

How to boost social-emotional development

Some of the following outbursts may be more typical among boys because boys tend to be more anxious about maintaining their status within a social hierarchy. But, as the following parent responses show, if you make your son's emotional welfare your first priority and respect his feelings, you will help him recognize and value the feelings in himself and others.

Michael "I hate school! The teacher shouted at me in front of my friends!"
Wrong "What did you do to make the teacher shout at you?"
Right "That must have been embarrassing for you."

George "I don't want him [visiting friend] to play with that toy. He can't have it!"
Wrong "You're a selfish child. You have to learn how to share."
Right "Sometimes it's hard to share a favorite toy. Let's put that toy away and take out some of the toys you feel more comfortable sharing."

Jamie "I don't like those boys. They're so mean. They won't play with me."
Wrong "If you weren't such a wimp and didn't make such a big deal out of every little thing, they would play with you."
Right "That must have hurt your feelings. Tell me what happened."

4 are boys the weaker sex?

4 Why are boys now in the news?

- **GIRLS GET EXTRA SCHOOL HELP WHILE BOYS GET RITALIN**
- **WARNING: MASCULINITY IS A DANGER TO HEALTH**
- **THE TROUBLE WITH BOYS**
- **THE FRAGILE MALE**
- **GOVERNMENT TACKLES BOYS' UNDERACHIEVEMENT**
- **LIFTING THE LID ON BOYS' DEPRESSION**
- **DELINQUENT MALES**

Those are the headlines – the actual words. You no doubt have seen similar ones, or worse. What is going on? Not so long ago, it was girls who were attracting all the attention. The concern was that, in many countries, girls are not given the chance to attend school, die in greater numbers than males due to inadequate health care and are treated by society as inferior. In developed countries, the outcry concerned girls not being encouraged enough to take up science or mathematics as well as unfair treatment at work.

Boy babies at risk

An American study involving more than 6,500 premature babies found death rates of 22 percent for boys compared with 15 percent for girls. However, giving steroids to mothers in premature labor helps to mature the lungs of their babies. Delivery by Caesarean section also helps to reduce breathing difficulties and brain trauma in these babies. They also found that the use of both these procedures had been more frequent among mothers of *girls*. And they found something else as well: breathing problems and brain injury were far more common in baby *boys*.

Now, it seems, the pendulum has swung the other way. Why? Is one sex really more vulnerable than the other, biologically speaking? Is one sex more at risk than the other because of society's gender expectations or stereotypes?

Underperforming boys

Around the world, boys are increasingly underachieving at school, particularly in reading. This is a relatively new phenomenon and one that is becoming more and more widespread. Although parents and teachers have been concerned about the trend for some time, it is now a topic that alarms government education officials and one to which the world's press frequently draws attention.

Speculation has centered on the idea that boys are biologically predisposed to underperform compared with girls. We are told that boys are at much higher risk than girls both before and after birth for everything from miscarriage to autism and from learning disabilities to dyslexia; that they lag behind girls developmentally. We are told that boys are far more likely to commit suicide, die in car accidents or be involved in violent crimes. In short, how could it have escaped our notice – it's not girls, but *boys* who are the weaker sex.

An accurate picture?

It would be convenient if we *could* categorize one sex as more vulnerable than the other, but there are a few troublesome points with the statistics.

○ The focus on rare diseases and events operates to exaggerate sex differences. (Although more boys than girls are autistic, American figures reveal that the overall incidence in the general population for both sexes combined is less than one in 1,000; some estimates are one in 2,000.)

○ The "boys are weaker" argument is selective in its reporting. Never included is the fact that teenage girls are twice as likely as boys to suffer from serious depression and are ten times more likely to suffer from eating disorders. Nor are we told that gifted boys significantly outperform gifted girls.

○ Many of the "facts" we are presented with are misleading. (While more males than females do kill themselves, females *try* to kill themselves seven times more often than males. Although dyslexia is *diagnosed* more often in boys than in girls, girls' reading problems more often go unnoticed.)

More alike than different

The truth is, as in all areas, boys and girls are really more alike than different. Although boys may be more vulnerable to injury before, during and just after birth, nature ensures that more boys than girls are conceived so that the ratio of males to females remains roughly equal. (In parts of the world where boys are awarded more status, the abortion of female fetuses has skewed the sex ratio in favor of males.)

Once they are born, the health and the emotional and intellectual development of girls and boys are equally vulnerable to environmental influences. Whether you have a boy or a girl, every child needs just as much attention, care and love as each other if they are to fulfill their potential.

4 The growing boy

When it comes to physicality of the sexes, it's obvious that boys are bigger and stronger than girls; females are definitely the weaker sex in this particular department. Girls are programmed to carry more body fat, whereas boys are destined to have more muscle tissue.

Boys' physical advantage is not there from the start, though, or at every stage of development. Around the ages of six to eight, girls are slightly shorter and lighter than boys, but by nine or ten the trend is reversed and girls begin to grow taller more rapidly. They continue to grow faster than boys until about thirteen and gain weight four times faster after sixteen. At thirteen, girls' height spurt is generally completed while boys' is in its early phase. By age fourteen, boys are, on average, taller than girls of the same age. And whereas girls grow no more than 2 inches (5 cm) after they reach puberty, boys often continue to grow until their early twenties. So, the average male is 6 inches (15 cm) taller than the average female. Meanwhile, their maximum period of weight gain (from twelve to sixteen) corresponds to their increasing height and muscle mass. Other physical differences between the sexes appear to affect the timing when certain bodily functions are mastered.

Did you know...?

Although babies of both sexes sleep for a similar amount of time to begin with, some evidence suggests that boy infants do not increase the amount of time they spend awake as quickly as girl babies do. Later on, nightmares (which occur during dream sleep) are common in both sexes, but occur more often in girls. Less common for both sexes are sleepwalking and night terrors (which occur while asleep but before dream sleep). Sleepwalking, which often runs in families, affects more boys than girls. These and other more minor problems usually disappear as children mature. Regular bedtime routines help to minimize common sleep problems.

Toilet-training

A child is usually physically ready to start toilet-training between eighteen months and two years old. The data from several countries shows that the average age for successful toilet-training is 27–28 months. Perhaps due to their physical differences, girls are often successful earlier than boys (average for girls is 26–27 months; for boys, 30 months or later).

Bed-wetting

During the first two or three years of life, bed-wetting at night is normal. At the age of five, at least 10–13 percent of children still wet the bed; on average, seven out of ten will be boys. The cause in over 90 percent of cases is an inherited tendency to abnormal patterns of sleep, making it difficult to awaken fully and respond to signals from the bladder. But a small bladder, lack of a hormone that inhibits urine production at night and muscular immaturity of the bladder may also contribute. Most children grow out of the problem by age of ten.

 How can I help my three-year-old son to stop wetting the bed at night?

A Wetting the bed at this age is very normal. Almost half of all children still wet the bed at the age of three. When your son has remained dry at night for three nights in a row, replace his diaper with underwear and tell him it's an experiment to see if it works. Use a plastic mattress protector for easier accident cleanup. Restrict fluids before bed and wake him before you go to bed for a last potty visit. If, after a few weeks of trying, he still wets the bed, reassure him by telling him his body is not ready yet. And return to training pants or diapers for a while.

Toilet-training tips

○ Buy a potty without a guard so that your son does not hurt himself and associate the potty with pain.

○ Begin training only when your son seems interested and willing.

○ Establish a regular pattern of toileting – upon rising, before and after meals, before bed.

○ Provide incentives (read him a story, sing a song or chat) to get him used to sitting still on his potty.

○ Provide plenty of praise and encouragement.

○ Remain calm and patient. Do not criticize or punish accidents.

○ Do not insist that your son remain seated longer than five to seven minutes.

○ Involve a willing male. Toddlers learn by imitation, so if he can watch a man or boy in the sitting down position it will work wonders.

○ Recruit an expert. Once your son has mastered the potty, recruit Dad or an older brother to help him learn about the standing position.

○ Sprinkle breakfast cereal or other flushable objects into the toilet bowl to encourage better targeting.

○ If at any point your son is not interested, do not push him.

4 Ear infections

About 80 percent of children have at least one episode of middle ear infection by the time they are three years old, but importantly, ear infections are more common among boys. Reasons for this could include boys' weaker immune systems and their more vulnerable inner ear anatomy (from birth, a part of the inner ear known as the cochlea is longer, and the semi-circular canals, in the balance system, are larger in diameter in boys).

Because ear infections can interrupt the normal development of important brain circuits, it is important to be ever alert. The worry is that even when an initial infection has cleared up, fluid can persist in the middle ear for several weeks, interfering with development. After an ear infection, be vigilant for any symptoms of hearing problem, such as unusual irritability, difficulty sleeping or pulling or tugging on his ears.

How can ear infections affect brain development?

Some ten years ago, researchers at the University of Sheffield, in the UK, found that dyslexic children or those with attention deficit hyperactivity disorder (ADHD), the majority of whom were boys, had difficulty performing balance tasks if asked to do something else at the same time. Their balance skills had not become fully automatic and still required conscious attention. It looked as though this deficiency was interfering with their ability to attend to other incoming signals, particularly auditory or visual information.

Many children with ADHD hear sounds as a bit of a jumble. It's not surprising, then, if they appear inattentive and lack concentration. Underlying balance difficulties may affect vision for some children with dyslexia.

Reading is tricky because the print seems to jump around on the page. Trying to process print symbols is like watching TV with a haywire vertical hold function.

In later research, it was found that a history of chronic ear infections, ear surgery or birth trauma was common among such children. This led the researchers to propose a theory. Recurrent ear problems can ultimately affect the normal course of development of the inner ear and balance or vestibular system. If inner ear development is interrupted enough, the neural circuits farther down the line

(to a part of the brain called the cerebellum and beyond) may not develop properly.

Recent brain-scanning studies involving children with dyslexia and ADHD provide convincing evidence that confirms this theory. It was found that these children's brains were underdeveloped in parts of the cerebellum. This part of the brain is important, as it receives all incoming signals (the inner ear's balance system affects how clearly these signals are received) – auditory, visual and kinesthetic (perception of body movements) and then relays this information on to the appropriate parts of the brain. Not only were parts of the cerebellum found to be underdeveloped, but the neural circuits between this region and the frontal control region (controlling impulsiveness and hyperactivity), and/or between this region and the brain region that converts letter symbols into sounds during reading were also poorly developed.

Keeping a check on your son's hearing

Since more boys than girls suffer from ear infections, it's important to have your son's hearing tested early if you have any concerns. Modern technology enables audiologists (the medical specialists of diagnosing hearing problems) to test the hearing of newborns and young children with great accuracy.

Schedule a hearing test if

○ your baby does not startle or jump in response to loud sounds;

○ your baby does not stop sucking or crying when there is a new sound;

○ your three-month-old baby does not coo at times or make eye contact when talked to;

○ your nine-month-old does not turn toward you when called from behind, or make babbling sounds such as "baba";

○ your one-year-old does not babble using a variety of consonant sounds (g, m, n, b, d);

○ your 18–20-month-old does not use single words to express his wants;

○ your two-year-old does not repeat words or phrases back to you and does not use short phrases when talking;

○ your son has had many ear infections;

○ your son uses gestures to communicate.

Unfortunately, many parents and doctors are unaware of these audiological tests. Parents concerned about their child's language development are often told to "wait and see," since "normal" development spans such a wide range. Most children with hearing loss don't have it diagnosed until after its initial onset, usually between the ages of two and three. This late diagnosis can result in significant delays in speech, language and brain development. It's imperative to act quickly.

4 Genetic health risks for boys

Every cell in a child's body has two chromosomes, and these genetic structures contain those all-important genes. Boys and girls differ in their chromosome quota. Remember those faster sperm carrying a Y chromosome? Since the mother's egg carries an X chromosome already, boys end up with an X and a Y (XY), whereas girls are XX.

Disadvantages of being XY

Females use only one of their X chromosomes at any one time; the other is "locked away" like a swimsuit in the winter. Evidence suggests that, as women grow older, their cells start to develop a preference for the stronger version. Males, however, don't have the option of choosing the higher-grade version of either the X or the Y because they get only one of each. So, if they are dealt a defective gene there is no chance of making a switch. This is why males are more prone to genetic disorders involving faulty genes on either the X or the Y chromosome.

Science has not yet worked out conclusively

which diseases and disorders are X-linked (linked to the mother's genes). It *is* known that fragile X syndrome, hemophilia and color blindness are X-linked, but for other disorders, such as asthma, autism and ADHD (see opposite), where it appears boys are more affected than

girls, no definite conclusions have yet been reached. Scientists do not know for certain to what extent these disorders stem from genetic or environmental causes or a combination of both.

X-linked diseases

These disorders (inherited from the mother on the X chromosome) are extremely rare, with the exception of red-green color blindness. Up to 8 percent of males may have a certain amount of trouble distinguishing red from green in some circumstances; only 0.5 percent of females are similarly affected. Color blindness is not a serious handicap, however, although some children may have to forgo their ambitions to become a commercial airline pilot.

Immune system disorders: ear infections, allergies, asthma

Males have less aggressive immune systems than females. This puts them at greater risk of infections such as dysentery, malaria and certain cancers. And perhaps this is another reason why boys tend to have more ear infections than girls (see page 80). Females, on the other hand, are more susceptible to illnesses caused by an overactive immune system, such as lupus, diabetes, ulcerative colitis and arthritis.

Although it is generally believed that allergies and hay fever are more common among boys than girls, a study investigating the incidence of asthma showed that age is a factor. From birth to the age of 23, 18–29 percent of the British population are affected by asthma. Before the age of seventeen it is more common among boys, but after this age it is slightly more common among girls. Asthma tends to run in families. Rather than being X-linked or related to weaker immunity in boys, therefore, it may simply be one of those diseases that either sex may inherit.

Autism

This developmental disorder affects the physical, social and language skills that usually appear during the first three years of life. Estimates of its occurrence range from 1 per 1,000 to 7 per 1,000 children. It is three or four times more common in boys than in girls. It is not yet known what causes autism, although there are many theories: some of these are related to boys' genetic risks and others are related to their weaker immune systems. Many avenues of research are being pursued. In one study, the risk of autism was estimated to be six times higher if the mother smoked during early pregnancy.

Attention deficit hyperactivity disorder (ADHD)

Almost all the behavior traits that characterize this disorder – inattentive, easily distracted, hyperactive, disruptive in class, won't stay in his seat, interrupts constantly – could describe the behavior of most normal boys, or, indeed, gifted boys (see box above).

The incidence of this disorder appears to be dependent upon cultural expectations. In the USA, for example, ADHD is diagnosed in 7 percent of children and three-quarters of them are treated using Ritalin, an amphetamine-like drug. In Britain, the incidence is reported to be less than 1 percent. Because ADHD is diagnosed in three to five times as many boys as girls, attempts have been made to prove a genetic link. This work has so far been inconclusive and, instead, much research points to environmental causes (ear infections are one probable cause – see page 81).

4 Food for thought: boost a boy's chances

Providing a healthful, balanced diet free from food additives, protecting against frequent use of antibiotics and breast-feeding your baby boy for as long as possible are all ways to enhance your son's physical, emotional and intellectual health and well-being.

Diet and boys' behavior

Some evidence suggests that diet can affect children's behavior. When children with ADHD (the majority were boys) were put on a multiple-item elimination diet, 73 percent responded favorably. When various high-

allergen foods (dairy products, wheat, corn, yeast, soya, beans, citrus, eggs, chocolate, peanuts) and foods containing artificial colors or preservatives were reintroduced, children behaved markedly worse.

A study involving primary-school children found that supplements of fish and plant oils could boost them from the bottom of the class to the top in just two terms. (Again, the majority involved were boys.) More than 40 percent of children showed improvements in their reading age, by as much as 1½–4½ years higher. Beware, though, that some fish can contain high levels of the metal mercury, which once it gets into the body is impossible to get rid of.

One way around this is to use oil extracted from sardines, as was done in this study. Such fish oil supplements can be bought from health food stores.

A link between food allergies and ear infections?

Children with ear infections are often treated with broad spectrum antibiotics. Antibiotics wipe out the friendly bacteria in the gut, which means that yeast, not normally a troublemaker, may begin to multiply. Overgrowth of yeast in the gut produces toxins that affect the nervous and immune systems. Additionally, changes in the flora in the digestive system can cause increased permeability of the gut, leading to greater risk of being affected by food allergies.

Why breast milk is sometimes especially good for boys

○ Breast-fed babies are only half as likely to get multiple ear infections as bottle-fed babies. (Boys are more vulnerable to ear infections than girls.)

○ Breast-fed children have IQs more than eight points higher at the age of eight than bottle-fed children whose mothers are similar in terms of education and socio-economic standing. (This is good for girls and boys.)

○ Thyroid hormone, present in breast milk, helps brain cells to survive and mature. (Boys are more vulnerable than girls to birth trauma.)

○ Variation in breast milk flavors plays an important role in taste development. (Boys may benefit from this stimulation to their senses more than girls, since testosterone is known to decrease sensitivity in a related area, the sense of smell.)

○ Breast-fed babies have fewer lung, stomach and urinary tract infections than bottle-fed babies since there is a large array of immune factors in breast milk. (Boys' immune systems are thought to be weaker than girls'.)

○ Taurine, an amino acid thought to play a special role in neural development, is present in breast milk. (It's beneficial for both boys' and girls' brain development.)

○ Breast milk contains more than 167 different types of fatty acids; such fats are essential to the process of myelination (see page 25). (Boys' brains develop more myelinated networks than girls', so they have an even greater need of these fatty acids.)

4 The typical male: image and reality

Violent, failing, lazy, irresponsible, unfeeling, "slow to talk and quick to shoot": are boys these days given unfair press? Their bad behavior is often blamed on testosterone or it's just attributed to their genes.

While female gender stereotypes have been changing rapidly, male stereotypes are still stuck in the past. Parents know that their boys do not actually fit the standard picture of what a male is supposed to be. They know that it is not unheard of for boys to be kind, gentle, clever, hardworking, witty, sensitive, helpful and clean (sometimes). The boys themselves are searching for an image of what masculinity should be. Much of what shapes their male behavior comes from observing (noticing gender roles, peers' behavior) and interacting with their environment (exposure to values of parents, peers, teachers). So, to what extent do boys deserve their rather negative reputation?

The insensitive male: are boys unfeeling?

The image
Boys are less sensitive, less emotional and less caring than girls are.

The reality
○ Both sexes feel emotions to the same extent, but society's stereotypes influence the ways they are displayed. When boys are emotional their parents may react in ways that say, "Tone it down." But boys can learn it's OK to show they're sad by watching their fathers cry; girls learn to be bolder by observing their mothers assert themselves.

○ Research shows that as gifted boys mature, feelings of hopefulness and encouragement increase. As gifted girls mature, however, they become subdued and their self-esteem nosedives.

The macho male: do boys take more risks?

The image
Boys are brave, strong and dominant. Assertive boys are labeled "leaders," whereas assertive girls are "bossy."

The reality
○ Risk-taking leading to accidents and injury is far more common among boys. (For girls, risk-taking may take the form of eating disorders.)

○ For boys, risk-taking is related to the need to establish dominance over a large group of males and gain social status. Risk-taking in girls is related to the need to establish social dominance over a small, high-status group of females; often it involves subtle verbal manipulation and maneuvers.

○ Gaining dominance is rated as one of the most important goals by 75 percent of boys; 80 percent of girls rate gaining intimacy as one of theirs.

○ More boys than girls injure themselves, die in road accidents or as a result of thrill-seeking activities. (More girls than boys suffer from depressive illness or die from eating disorders.)

The tough male: are boys involved in more sex, crime and violence?

The image
Boys are testosterone-driven, physically aggressive and less mature than girls socially and emotionally.

The reality
- Both sexes learn to be violent by experiencing it firsthand. The influences of peer pressure and negative gender roles are reduced in the teen years if parents provide positive, perhaps atypical, role models when children are young.
- Aggression is not caused by testosterone. Aggressive behavior (physical or verbal) is brought on by family conflict, weak bonds with family and friends, low grades in primary school, poor social skills, disadvantaged neighborhood and a lack of praise; all such factors affect boys more than girls.
- Boys' distress may erupt as oppositional behavior; this elicits negative reactions and boys' negative behavior escalates. Ten times as many boys are involved in violent crimes as girls. (Girls' distress is often internalized; they may dwell on problems, and become depressed, lose confidence or turn their anger on themselves. Twice as many teenage girls as boys suffer serious depressive illness.)
- A third of boys (and a quarter of girls) have their first sexual encounter before they reach sixteen years of age.
- The incidence of sexually transmitted infections in teenage boys ranges from less than 1 percent to 10 percent. Up to 33 percent of teenage girls have herpes and 2 percent have genital warts.

The data that follows comes from a large survey of over 14,000 youths aged eleven to seventeen in England, Wales, and Scotland.

- 17.5 percent of seven-year-old boys engage in bullying (16 percent of girls); at fourteen, 6.4 percent of boys are bullies (3 percent of girls).
- 40 percent of 14–15-year-olds (equal numbers of boys and girls) had ever been involved in small acts of vandalism or shoplifting.
- 10 percent of 16-year-old boys had been involved in burglary (far fewer girls).
- 8–19 percent of boys (depending on age) admit to attacking someone or carrying a weapon (very few girls are involved in violent crimes).

The irresponsible male? Smoking, drugs, alcohol...

The image
Boys are viewed as more irresponsible than girls, but is this really the case? Do boys really deserve this derogatory label?

The reality
These are some more of the findings from the survey mentioned above.
- Smoking is more prevalent among all girls in the age range; 29 percent of girls and 22 percent of boys smoke on a regular basis.
- Alcohol consumption is very common among both boys and girls, with 80 percent of sixteen-year-olds drinking on a regular basis.
- Approximately 30 percent of boys smoke cannabis (compared with 25 percent of girls).
- The reported use of illegal drugs is relatively low for both sexes; about 5 percent of boys and 4 percent of girls said they had used Ecstasy.
- More girls than boys said they missed whole days of school or longer (18 percent versus 16 percent).

For both sexes, protective factors include healthy standards set by parents and school, friends who are not involved in these activities and good achievement in primary school.

4 Boys' self-esteem

A healthy self-concept is vital to both boys and girls if they are to make the most of their potential. Changes during puberty and the amount of success experienced at school are two factors that can wreak havoc with a child's self-confidence. Although girls' self-esteem can suffer as a result of these influences, there are puberty-related and school issues (see Chapter 6) that are specific to boys. These have the potential to make them feel as if they might be the "weaker sex."

Concerns of teenage boys

The testosterone-triggered changes in puberty can make boys feel especially vulnerable. Here are some common concerns and how you can help.

Early or late puberty

There is huge variation as to when boys enter puberty, but all boys want desperately to be the same as others. Although the whole process is very gradual, usually four or five years, a boy who begins puberty seriously ahead of others may feel more conspicuous. Probably worse is the boy who lags considerably

behind other boys. He may despair that, while all the other boys around him are gradually turning into men, there he is, still looking like a child.

What to do Try to be sensitive to your son's concerns without being overly intrusive. Help to provide him with the opportunity to become involved in a sport that he enjoys and suits his body type. Be tolerant of his ravenous appetite (have plenty of healthful, high-energy foods on hand) and his alternating periods of high and low activity.

Appearance

In childhood, boys compete with each other largely in the sporting arena. During the early teens, however, there is a new competition. Forming relationships with girls suddenly becomes another route to gaining status in the eyes of other boys. Although it is probably the rare boy who does not worry about some aspect of his appearance (ears too big, nose too long, bad skin, voice too high, not enough beard, not big enough penis, too short, too thin, too fat, not enough muscle and so on), these worries are not always something a boy wants to air with his parents. Boys constantly check each other out at this stage and, if comfortable, may commiserate with each other.

What to do Respect your son's privacy but be open to conversation about his concerns if he asks you.

Stages of puberty: the potential ego-wreckers

AGE (YEARS)	
11–13	More frequent erections, with or without stimulation.
11–14	Hair begins to grow on face and body.
11–15	Vocal cords grow longer and thicker; voice becomes lower.
12–13	Sperm production stimulated; first wet dreams.
12–13	Muscle mass increases.
12–14	Spurt in height and weight (on average, two years later than girls).
12–14	Oil glands become more active; may lead to skin problems.
12–17	Hormones cause abrupt emotional fluctuations.
13–15	Penis and scrotum grow to adult size over a two-year period.

Parents' attitudes

The young teenage boy tends to see himself as three years older than he actually is. His parents, on the other hand, tend to see him as three years younger! This creates a problem. There is almost nothing more mortifying for a boy at this stage than to have his parents come to watch him play a game of football, for instance, then sidle up to him afterward and begin, in front of his friends, to tidy his hair.

What to do Treat your son like a grown-up – especially in front of his friends. Make him feel that you trust him to stick to clearly laid-down rules and to behave responsibly. If he breaks the rules, encourage *him* to make decisions about what should be done. Your son will have greater confidence in himself if he sees that you believe in him.

Sexual orientation

It is likely to be a matter of great anguish to your son if he feels that he is gay. If he is simply attracted to other boys, it does not necessarily mean that he is gay. Young boys like other boys and admire their own bodies. Girls may be viewed as scary. Adolescents today are also bombarded with confusing media messages about sexuality and young pubertal boys may not be mature enough to process what they are seeing and hearing appropriately.

What to do If your son tells you he thinks he is gay, put *his* emotional needs first and let him know that you still love him. If you have a healthy attitude toward accepting him as he is, it will help him sort out his own sexuality and teach him tolerance for others' sexual orientation.

5 boys in motion

5 Developmental strides

Robert watches proudly as his son Jonathan crawls at speed after the ball disappearing into the corner. He'll be walking soon! And, suddenly, he sees a vision of the future – his son grown strong and muscular, a famous football player… His reverie is cut short when a friend arrives with her daughter Emily. Once Emily is put down on the floor, Robert watches as she crawls over to the sofa, hoists herself up and proceeds to cruise along its edge. And then – she lets go. She's walking! Robert knows that Emily is younger than Jonathan at just ten months old. Why, he wonders, is my one-year-old son so far behind?

Babies' increasing ability to use their muscles purposefully to move around and to coordinate different parts of their bodies – their motor progress – is the most obvious sign of brain development. But should parents worry that their son is not yet walking when other, younger children are? No, they shouldn't. Studies show that a baby's motor development has little to do with later physical abilities. Just because

Jonathan is not yet walking, it does not mean he won't be a star center-forward one day.

The most striking thing about children's motor development is how predictable it is. Babies the world over, whatever their culture, seem to acquire motor skills in the very same consistent sequence.

Although children do not vary in the *sequence* of milestones achieved, they can vary widely in the speed

Kinds of motor development

Motor skills are divided into two types, gross and fine. Gross motor skills involve the coordination of large muscles of the body, the arms and the legs. Fine motor skills are those that require the coordination and manipulation of the smaller muscles of the hands and arms. Related to motor skills is balance, which involves the ability to sense movement and perceive where your body is in space. This is necessary in maintaining head and body posture and hugely influences the course of motor development.

at which they achieve them. So unless a child is especially slow, dramatically behind the normal ranges, there is no reason at all for concern.

When it comes to the first year of life, though, studies show that baby boys and girls (in spite of widespread individual variation) accomplish the various motor milestones at a similar rate. One U.S. study showed that baby boys' motor development was in advance of baby girls' during the first three months of life, but that for the remainder of that first year, the sexes did not differ in their motor prowess.

Is motor development related to mental development?

Research studies have found no direct correlation between a child's early motor abilities and IQ score, but motor skills do encourage and assist mental development.

Every time a baby reaches a new milestone, a new learning opportunity awaits him. Once your baby boy can reach out and grasp an object, he can then go on to learn how it feels, how it sounds or how it tastes. Once he begins crawling, he encounters new things to explore and new people with whom to interact. Each and every new motor milestone exposes him to new experiences, giving him a whole new perspective on the world.

While your child's muscles are becoming stronger and better coordinated, he grows not only intellectually, but emotionally as well. You will have noticed how obviously pleased he is with himself when he succeeds with a new motor skill. One spin-off of such accomplishments is a dramatic boost to his self-esteem and his growing sense of independence.

5 First moves

A baby will already have had seven or eight months of physical exercise moving around in the womb, so perhaps it stands to reason that the motor areas of the brain are among the first to show electrical activity among newborns. In fact, fetal movements are the single most important form of brain stimulation the fetus receives.

In spite of this early start, the newborn has a long way to go. Motor circuits in the brain are incredibly complex, developing slowly from the bottom to the top, from lower brain regions to higher areas. All babies' movements thus progress from primitive and reflexive to more purposeful, from being able to control central parts of the body (head and torso) to peripheral body parts (hands and limbs).

In the higher brain areas, neural growth proceeds from the bottom to the top, too. In terms of the

Motor milestones during the first year

AVERAGE AGE	GROSS MOTOR SKILL	FINE MOTOR SKILL
0		Reflexive grasp
1–2 MONTHS	Begins to hold head up	
2–3 MONTHS	Starts to lift head and chest if on tummy and can sit with support	
3 MONTHS		Purposeful grasp
3–4 MONTHS	Begins to roll from tummy to back	
4–5 MONTHS		Successful at reaching and grasping
6–7 MONTHS	Begins to roll from back on to tummy	Has control when reaching and grasping
6–8 MONTHS	Can sit unaided	
8–9 MONTHS	Can pull to stand	
9 MONTHS	Able to crawl	Grasps with thumb and forefinger
9–10 MONTHS	Can walk with handholds ("cruises")	
10 MONTHS		Claps his own hands
9–12 MONTHS		Transfers toy from one hand to the other
11–12 MONTHS	Can stand unsupported	
12–13 MONTHS	Starts to walk unaided	
12–14 MONTHS		Can let go of objects on purpose

muscles controlled, this means from head to toe. Babies master head and facial movements (smiling) before arm movements (reaching and grasping), which, in turn, are mastered before leg movements (crawling and walking).

A balancing act

All that moving around in the womb means that the balance or *vestibular* system is remarkably mature at birth. Amazingly, the vestibular nerve is the very first neural network in the whole brain to begin to insulate itself with white matter or myelin, just five months after gestation. The early maturity of this system explains why babies almost seem to crave, and are soothed by, repetitive motion. They love to be rocked, jiggled, bounced, carried around or, later on, spun, swung, flipped upside down or given "plane rides."

Even though relatively mature at birth, the vestibular system needs stimulation not only to refine its networks but also to boost the proper development of the neural networks linking it to higher brain regions. The chair-spinning experiment described in Chapter 1 (see page 29) showed that this stimulation resulted in speedier brain development.

The brain's "air-traffic control"

In a hollow opening in the skull (the vestibule) is the inner ear, which houses two kinds of balance (or vestibular) organs. Neural networks travel from these to a number of brain regions, which use the information they receive to coordinate movement. For example,

○ eyes use messages from the vestibular organs to adjust eye movements so that the images the eyes see are stable;

○ the spinal cord uses the information to control posture and the position of the arms and legs.

Neural networks also extend directly from the inner ear organs to an important region at the back of the brain, the cerebellum.

Did you know ...?

Babies relish movement. So strong is their desire for it that up to 15 percent help their vestibular or balance systems to develop by providing their *own* self-stimulation. At around six to eight months of age, these babies may be seen rocking back and forth or banging their heads repeatedly against the wall. In an investigation of this phenomenon, it was found that babies who were body rockers and head bangers reached various motor milestones much earlier than other babies. Perhaps boy babies have an even stronger need for this kind of stimulation than girls, as boy "head bangers" outnumbered girls three to one.

The cerebellum has a very tricky job as it is essentially the brain's "air-traffic control" system. It not only receives information from the various senses about what kind of movement is taking place (vision, hearing, and balance) but also receives messages from the higher brain's motor regions, which tell it what kind of movement the body is attempting to make. By comparing all this information, it directs the body to produce precisely timed, coordinated body movements. The cerebellum is only one-tenth the size of the whole brain, but in order to handle its mammoth amount of work it contains one-*half of all* the brain's nerve cells.

5 Does practice make perfect?

Like all brain development, the development of motor skills involves a delicate dance between nature and nurture. There is constant interaction between the growth and maturation of motor pathways in the brain and the consistent exercise a baby or young child puts himself or herself through on a daily basis.

It is only relatively recently that scientists have changed their views on babies' motor development. Research conducted in the 1930s and '40s concluded that motor development depends solely on the maturation of muscles and neural networks in the brain. It was thought that practice and experience made no difference whatsoever.

But whereas early researchers were focused on how similar babies were, recent investigators have examined some of their differences. They discovered that motor development is not wholly a matter of waiting for the right neural circuits to wire up according to some genetic blueprint. In fact, babies can improve their motor skills with diligent practice, much as adults can.

Some recent findings

The following are just some of the interesting findings from this research:

○ Blind babies are less motivated to develop their locomotor skills. Unable to see people or interesting objects, they are delayed in reaching for objects, crawling and walking.

○ Researchers found that lying on their backs does not allow babies to exercise their arm and neck muscles as much as tummy-lying, and babies who spent a lot of time on their backs were slower to roll over, sit, crawl and pull to stand. Because current advice to minimize the risk of crib death (SIDS) is to put young babies to sleep on their backs, when they are awake they should get as much opportunity as possible for "tummy time."

○ Training one twin does not accelerate the mastery of skills like walking or stair-climbing, but it does end up increasing that twin's confidence and interest in motor skills compared with an untrained sibling. Although enthusiastic parents who encourage their baby to practice specific movements may not affect the timing of their child's motor milestones, the movements themselves will ultimately help that child succeed at physical activities.

○ Although motor pathways are primitive and instinct-based to begin with, they grow and become more complex through use. The more these developed pathways are activated during consistent, purposeful action, the likelier they are to become permanent. Imaging studies in adults show that when a person becomes skilled at a certain motor task, such as a sequence of finger movements, a larger area in their brain is involved during this task than before training.

○ Babies brought up in certain traditional cultures (African, Indian and Latin American) tend to develop motor skills more rapidly than those brought up in westernized societies. It is thought this is because parents in industrialized countries rely more on equipment to carry or contain their babies while they do daily chores. Mothers in traditional cultures, however, often carry their babies in slings for most of the day, forcing their babies' brains to work harder to maintain balance and support their heads, stimulating both motor and vestibular development.

○ Training alters the way the motor pathways in the brain both develop and are later refined. Repeated practice results in larger areas within the higher brain regions being activated than before a skill becomes well learned. As certain skills, such as crawling and walking, for example, become more and more expert and automatic, the degree to which the cerebellum, the "air-traffic control" system in the lower, more primitive brain, is activated, *decreases*. This is a great step forward! This means that the cerebellum is freed up to a considerable extent and is better able to concentrate on other tasks that have not yet become fully automatic.

Q **Is it a good idea to encourage my son to walk from an early age?**

A Practice is essential to your son's motor progress but it needs to happen at the right time. If it occurs too early, the necessary neural circuits may not yet be in place and your son will be unable to benefit from it. In fact, he may become frustrated trying to do something that he has no chance of accomplishing at that stage. However, as long as he seems interested, encourage him to keep trying. Evidence shows that babies who keep reaching for an object, for example, succeed at grasping a few weeks earlier than babies who use their arms less.

5 Where boys and girls *do* differ

Boys spend more time than girls engaged in locomotor activity – that is, trying to get from A to B – whether it's by crawling, bottom-shuffling, walking, running, lunging or plunging. From the time they're born, boys tend to be more curious about exploring the physical space around them and seem to enjoy rough-and-tumble play more than baby girls do.

Boy babies are physically stronger, lifting their heads higher when lying down and actively moving their whole bodies more. They tend to excel in those skills requiring power and force. Their larger muscle mass means that, even by the age of five, they can jump farther, run faster and throw a ball farther than girls of the same age can. Their coordination in throwing a ball overarm and side-armed is better developed and, generally, they learn earlier how to ride a two-wheeled bicycle.

Girls, on the other hand, tend to be better than boys in some motor skills requiring balance and coordination, such as jumping, hopping and skipping. They also tend to be better at performing some fine motor tasks such as manipulating buttons or fastenings. Why is this? Success at fine motor skills requires attention and perceptual ability. Because girls tend to be more anxious to please than boys, this may be why they generally succeed earlier than boys in tasks that parents show most interest in – feeding themselves, using scissors and tying their shoelaces, for example.

These differences, however, are slight. Many boys and girls will reach the major milestones at roughly the same time, and among both boys and girls there is wide variation. Remember, of course, that there are just as many children succeeding *after* the average age as before. So if your son leads or lags behind the milestones listed at right by several weeks or months, this is entirely normal.

What explains these differences?

These sex differences in motor development are a reflection of what is happening inside the brains of each sex. Until about the age of six, boys' brains (probably due to evolutionary reasons) are primarily focused on building and refining the neural networks associated with visual-spatial discrimination, planning gross motor movements, visual targeting and accessing stored information. The neural circuits in boys' brains that handle fine motor skills grow, too, but at a slower rate.

Girls' brains at this time give top priority to the development of the neural networks associated with language processing, visual matching involving fine details, fine motor skills and social behavior. For boys, during the first six years, a larger part of neural growth takes place in the brain's right hemisphere. For girls, however, early brain development is skewed in favor of the left hemisphere.

With this in mind, there is absolutely no reason to be concerned if your daughter was able to thread beads on a string at the age of three, whereas your son appears to be completely unable to accomplish this task when he is four. Boys and girls catch up with each other in their ability to perform fine and gross motor skills. It is simply a case of having brains with different agendas.

Some more milestones

By the following ages, half of all children can

	BOYS	GIRLS
Gross motor skills		
jump in place	2 yrs 5 mths	2 yrs 4 mths
jump off a stair	2 yrs 9 mths	2 yrs 8 mths
hop on one foot	4 yrs	3 yrs 10mths
throw beanbag (overhand)	4 yrs 5 mths	5 yrs 5 mths
catch a beanbag	4 yrs 5 mths	5 yrs 5 mths
Fine motor skills		
use a spoon	1 yr 10 mths	1 yr 6 mths
use a fork	2 yrs 8 mths	2 yrs 4 mths
do/undo buttons	3 yrs 5 mths	3 yrs
use scissors	4 yrs	3 yrs 5 mths
tie shoelaces	5 yrs	4 yrs 5 mths
cut with a knife.	6 yrs 5 mths	6 yrs

as great as those seen on spatial rotation tasks (see page 17). But since this ability is not related to boys' performance on spatial rotation tests, researchers have concluded that it is an entirely separate ability and requires another kind of skill – rapid spatio-motor analysis.

Experiments reveal that this difference appears very early in life, at the age of three to five, when boys and girls do not differ greatly in muscle bulk or strength, or in the amount of targeting experiences they are likely to have had.

Brain imaging studies have now helped to explain these findings. From birth until the age of six, boys' brains develop unique "visual tracking" neural networks, linking motor areas with visual areas. Girls, on the other hand, do not develop similar circuits until after the age of eight.

Hitting the target

One of the largest, most reliable sex differences that has been found involves accuracy in a motor activity that probably evolved from the earliest of times – that is, aiming at a target.

The differences between girls and boys in throwing accurately or in intercepting an object are

Looking at the facts behind the statistics

Most of us have the preconception that when it comes to fine motor skills, girls do better, and that with gross motor skills, boys are the star performers. But this is not always the picture that emerges. When we look at how certain findings were arrived at, we discover that factors such as the method of measurement or the age of the sample chosen can affect the results.

A science fair surprise

In a school science fair project, the fine motor skills of pupils and teachers were assessed with a specially designed machine. The testers expected to find that the girls (aged between six and twelve) would outperform boys of the same ages, but that the male and female teachers would be equal in ability.

To their surprise, they discovered that, although the six-year-old girls were superior to boys, the twelve-year-old boys and the male teachers came out ahead of their female counterparts in performing this fine motor task.

What do these results mean? They may merely indicate that the particular way fine motor skills were measured in this instance led to the results obtained. Or they may mean that although boys' fine motor skills lag behind girls to begin with, later on they surpass girls in this area.

Method of measurement

How a specific motor skill is measured makes a critical difference in the results of that research. For example, in one study, it was found that girls and boys aged between four and six did not differ in their throwing accuracy. By contrast, in a separate study, boys were found to be significantly better than girls at all ages from four to fourteen in their ability to throw with accuracy. When we look in detail at the methods used for the studies, we find that in the first study children had to throw underarm whereas in the second they had to throw overarm.

At all ages girls and boys do not differ overall in their balancing skills. But differences emerge when specific tasks are measured. Skipping, for instance, is usually accomplished earlier by girls than boys, but kicking or riding a bicycle are things boys do much better or earlier than girls.

A number of studies investigating children's fine motor skills have found no sex differences in the time taken for girls and boys to place, rotate or turn over pegs in a board. However, they were allowed to use whichever hand they liked, or both hands. But in a study in which researchers narrowed down the task by instructing the children to use either their dominant or their non-dominant hand, girls were found to be quicker than boys when using their dominant hand.

This last finding probably has something to do with the fact that girls are quicker to establish a dominant hand than boys. At birth, for example, boys' lower body reflexes are *left-biased* (indicating their right hemispheres are dominant), whereas girls' reflexes are *right-biased* (indicating their left hemispheres are dominant). By the age of three, however, both girls and boys will have established a dominant hand. Most (85–90 percent) will be right-handed, about 2 percent more being females.

Age of the children involved

Apart from throwing and ball-handling skills, gender differences in gross motor performance during

childhood are very slight. Differences become much more apparent during adolescence, and largely favor boys. Data from large-scale studies show that from eleven to seventeen years of age, girls' running and jumping performance improves 2–7 percent, whereas improvement in boys ranges from 18 to 36 percent.

Did you know... ?

Babies in Mexico of both sexes are better than babies in the USA at fine motor skills. And boys in Switzerland from the ages of five to eighteen are just as adept at sequential finger movements, a fine motor task, as girls.

5 How to enhance your son's motor skills

If you are athletic, does it increase your son's chances of following in your footsteps? Genes probably determine motor performance to a much greater extent than most of us think. Studies of twins show that inherited characteristics can determine anywhere from 20 to 75 percent of a person's motor performance. And it seems that the environment and any physical training are also influential.

Studies that have examined the effects of training suggest that heredity accounts for about 50 percent (estimates for runners range from 45 to 92 percent), outside influences about 42 percent and interaction between the two 8 percent. So, while a certain amount of what influences your children's physical aptitude is beyond your control, there is plenty of scope within the environment they experience to boost their talents.

Breast milk
Mothers in Taiwan who received a high-calorie and high-protein supplement during pregnancy and the first eight months of their child's life while breast-feeding produced babies who were no smarter than those of non-supplemented mothers. But, consistent with the findings of two other large-scale nutritional studies, the *motor* scores of the "supplement" babies, regardless of sex, were higher.

However, breast-feeding, with or without a dose of supplements, has been shown to have a beneficial effect on many aspects of a baby's growth, including motor progress. Mothers from traditional societies, such as in Africa and India, tend to breast-feed their babies for longer, and this has been shown to contribute to their accelerated acquisition of motor skills. See also page 97.

Factors known to influence the rate of motor development

Social class Motor milestones were examined in a large number of Pakistani babies aged 0 to 24 months. There were no sex differences but infants from the poorer classes were three months later in their walking and fine motor activities.

Environment Walking is often delayed by factors such as restrictive clothing, slippery cold floors, excessive body weight or an overly protective environment.

Diet Over 1,500 Danish babies' motor milestones were assessed during their first year of life. The proportion of babies who mastered specific milestones increased consistently (regardless of sex) with increasing duration of breast-feeding.

Q I am pregnant and expecting a boy. Can my exercise regimen make a difference in my son's motor skills?

A If you are naturally athletic, then your son may well inherit those characteristics. However, in one study, mothers who continued regular, sustained, vigorous exercise throughout pregnancy had lighter babies with less subcutaneous fat, regardless of their sex.

At five years of age, the height of the children who had been "exercise babies" was found to be similar to those who had been "non-exercise babies" but the "exercise" children still weighed less. Motor skills and school readiness were found to be similar in both groups, but the "exercise" group had higher IQ scores.

Bringing out the explorer instinct

Encourage your son to explore all the spaces around him – both inside the home and outdoors – as this will help him learn more and, at the same time, boost his self-confidence in venturing farther afield. See also page 97 for examples of how practicing movements can help development.

Improving those fine motor skills

When children start school, much of the day's activity suddenly seems to involve controlling a pencil or paintbrush. Because these are fine motor skills, boys in particular can find them troublesome and can get very frustrated by any ineptitude.

Anything that requires finger manipulation can help improve your son's fine motor control. Play dough or modeling clay can provide excellent practice. These can be squashed, rolled and shaped into almost any object your son desires.

Building toys that link together can also be very helpful. Large paintbrushes, felt pens and chalk are easier to use than an ordinary-size pencil and can help build your son's confidence. Other toys that can accelerate fine motor skills include piggy banks, toy cash registers and nuts and bolts.

Look for games such as join-the-dots books, or try drawing your own sequence of treasure hunt dots for your son to follow, letting him join them as he goes, using his own chosen drawing instrument. At the end of the route, give him a treat. Draw a sequence of dots in the shape of an object for him to connect and guess what the object is. As long as computer games do not monopolize all your son's free time, they, too, are helpful in developing hand-to-eye coordination. Finally, encourage only those things that your son wants to do and finds fun.

5 Sports

Most boys become involved in sports for the simple reason that it is fun. It is said that there is a sport to suit any boy, from karate to kite-flying, from hockey to hiking, from cricket to croquet and from football to Frisbee throwing. But more than being just a fun pastime, sports can benefit your son in myriad ways: building his self-confidence, social skills, and powers of concentration as well as his physical prowess.

Why are sports so appealing to boys?

Whether it's surfing, relay running, basketball or games of tennis-ball tag on the playground, sports hold particular appeal for boys. This is because boys have a natural inclination to

○ move their bodies a lot;

○ explore the physical spaces around them;
○ experiment with different ways of maneuvering their bodies in space;
○ excel in gross motor and ball-handling skills;
○ aim at a physical target (by throwing, kicking, shooting, catching, and intercepting objects with hands, head, or feet)
○ work at establishing and maintaining their social status in the eyes of other males;
○ form competitive male groups;
○ develop hierarchies within a male group.

Because boys are essentially biologically programmed to be talented in all these areas, such activities tend to be activities that they particularly enjoy. As boys practice these skills they become even more accomplished; and so begins a cycle of more effort for more pleasure, leading to increased motivation to practice further for more reward, and so on. The satisfaction that comes from working hard and mastering a skill is exhilarating. While boys are engaged in exercise or sports they experience this thrill on almost a moment-to-moment basis.

Even if a boy's interest in sports is simply because it is fun, his instincts are on the right track – having fun imparts a sense of emotional well-being and will increase his receptivity to learning.

The many benefits of sports

Research shows that exercise and participation in sports can lead to the following benefits:

○ Enhanced physical fitness and well-being. Exercise helps to build strong bones and muscles, and to improve strength, motor skills and athletic ability.

○ Enhanced emotional growth and social skills. Sports provide opportunities for boys to experience pride and joy in their physical skillfulness and to feel special when their father or another male role model spends time with them. Participating in sports, especially team sports, makes a boy feel worthy and successful, and accepted by other males as well as teaching him how to deal with feelings of disappointment.

○ Enhanced social skills. It can provide a boy, from a young age, the opportunity for special male bonding time with his father or stepfather. Boys can learn how to work with others as a team, and how to interact appropriately with peers and with adults.

○ Increased energy levels and powers of concentration. Exercise can improve the ability to persevere with a task and to achieve goals; it can reduce hyperactivity, distractibility, and attention and behavioral problems in the classroom.

○ Improved brain function. Regular exercise increases blood flow to the brain, which enhances nutrient intake and raises the levels of various substances in the brain that maintain the health of neurons. Learning the rules and processes involved in sports assists the ability to retain information.

○ Good balance, coordination and timing abilities. Exercise helps to improve rhythmic abilities and efficient functioning of the cerebellum (the brain's "air-traffic control" system). The ability to see, hear and balance in an automatic and unconscious fashion has been found to determine overall school achievement, including mathematics and reading ability.

○ Reduced incidence of drug and alcohol abuse. Children who participate in sports are less likely to start smoking in the first place, but if they do smoke, they are more likely to quit.

○ Reduced inappropriate social behavior. Juveniles at high risk for violence and delinquency were less resistant to rules, less impulsive, and less violent after participating in a martial arts course.

○ Enhanced moral development. Learning to abide by the rules and play fairly helps boys learn to distinguish right from wrong.

Are sports built into boys' brains?

We have seen that, from the time they are born, boys are more active than girls. This difference is likely to result from hormonal influences – the same ones that determine brain structure and function. Boys' brains drive them to want to compete with one another, and to facilitate this, they get together in groups and create social hierarchies.

A perfect illustration is the game Ultimate. This game was invented in Maplewood, New Jersey, when a group of boys were fooling around in the high school parking lot, throwing a Frisbee. After they evolved their own rules for a team game, the game spread rapidly across the USA and is now played in 42 countries around the world.

Boosting precious self-esteem

Because exercise can take many forms, whether team games or more solitary pursuits, the opportunity exists for all boys to find a sport or physical activity that suits them and to experience the satisfaction of achievement in one area of their lives. In the same way that sports heroes are idolized by our society – and also *because* they are – as a boy gains more skill and knowledge in a sport, he, too, gains greater respect from those in his immediate social surroundings. His confidence, self-esteem and social status all receive a significant boost.

However, just as sports can offer positive benefits – a chance for openness, expression and intimacy – sports can also push boys into loneliness, shame and

Good and bad at sports

Although some studies find an association between achievement in sports and academic attainment, there are a number of other studies that demonstrate that balancing the amount of time spent in each endeavor is key. One English study found that the more time children aged thirteen to sixteen devoted to sports, the worse their English and science scores tended to be.

vicious competition. It can be the trigger for unbridled aggression, inappropriate feelings of anger and frustration and physical hurt to others. These are, of course, all damaging to self-esteem and ruin a boy's enjoyment. The benefits of sports cease when it stops being play. If a boy is not enjoying a sport, he should stop and find some form of sports he does enjoy.

How important is achievement in the physical domain to boys' overall self-concept? A recent UK study addressed this very question. Almost 400 pupils aged thirteen to fifteen were asked to rate how important success in sports and success in schoolwork was to them. It turned out that all pupils rated academic success as more important than sports success. Boys, however, thought that success in sports was more important than girls did. Other research has also shown that children with the highest academic achievement score the highest on measures of self-esteem.

Sports: are there any disadvantages?

Physical exercise and involvement with sports provide an enormous category of benefits to boys. Are there any harmful effects? Is there a downside?

The risk of injury is probably of most concern to parents. According to a survey of hospital emergency data in Wales, sports injuries are on the rise. For boys aged ten to fifteen, the risk of injury from sports

Q Are boys bad at losing? How can I help my son handle disappointment?

A How your son deals with the stress of winning or losing a game depends in large part upon you (or his coach). Try to talk to your son at home after a game, not on the sidelines or on the way to and from a game or practice. Focus specifically on something positive your son did during the game, even if his team was beaten badly. He will enjoy the idea that he might have accomplished something during the game that was worth remembering and discussing with you. If your son performed poorly and realizes it, help him work through his disappointment by talking about what he has learned from the experience and how he will be able to play better in the next game. Boys are amazingly resilient to tough losses, and you may well find that your son bounces back from a loss much faster than you do.

increased from just 1 percent in 1983 to 5 percent in 1998. According to a Scottish survey, 71 percent of children injured through sports are boys, football being the most common sport implicated. However, to keep this in perspective, most of children's injuries are not serious. In the Welsh study, for example, only two out of five sports injuries were involved bone fractures. This translates to an overall risk of only 1.4 percent of a boy in Wales sustaining a serious injury from sports.

Nevertheless, whatever sport your son is interested in or involved with, always be aware of anything you can do to make that particular sport a safer activity – from modification of rules to the use of specialized safety equipment or additional expert coaching.

6 education

6 New, worldwide underachieving boys

John and Rachel are anxiously trying to decide which pre-school their little three-year-old "genius," George, ought to attend. It is so difficult to choose. Questions loom. He can recite the alphabet and count to ten but perhaps they ought not to have taught him these things? And yet, the newspapers are full of stories about boys' underachievement in reading. How can they make sure their son does well at school?

Girls' underachievement in mathematics and science was once the main concern, but now it is the boys who are attracting all the attention. While it is certainly true that the greater encouragement girls have been receiving may be contributing to a closing gender gap in mathematics and science, this is not the whole story. There is something else afoot. Boys are behind at every level, in almost every school subject. By the end of the primary or elementary years, many boys are beginning to lose interest in school. They are three times more likely than girls to have behavioral problems. Later, as teenagers, far more boys than girls decide to drop out of school altogether. At the university level, enrollment is increasingly female. In some institutions, females now outnumber males by two or three to one. What is happening?

Does a late start help?

A Canadian study found that entrance age is not a good predictor of a child's academic progress. No differences were found in the amount of progress younger and older first-year children made. In spite of their age differences, they learned at an equivalent rate. The younger children, in fact, learned at a far faster rate than their same-age mates who were attending pre-school, one year below.

By the middle school years, age exerts even less of an influence on performance. A 1989 Israeli study (involving over 12,000 pupils) found that the number of years a child had spent in school had far more impact on IQ than chronological age. Young year 5 (grade 5) pupils were found to score within a point or two of the older children in their classes, but their IQ scores were some *five points higher* than children of roughly the same age who were in the school year below.

What these and other studies demonstrate is that what a child gains by being among the oldest in the class is more than offset by how much he loses by missing a whole year of school.

Making boys successful

Many varied theories have been put forward to account for this worrisome state of affairs, and many remedies suggested to cure it. One popular argument is that boys are slower to mature and would therefore benefit from starting their formal education later than girls. Age, however, has very little influence on performance, and a delayed start is more likely to harm than help a child attain his or her intellectual potential (see box opposite).

Other factors – ethnic group, gender, socio-economic background – are known to exert more influence. However, research shows that there is just one important factor that can overcome all these in predicting your son's academic success: reading.

Reading – are schools failing boys?

A large survey conducted by the University of London in 1993, which followed 800 pupils over nine years, showed that the single most important factor predicting the academic achievement of sixteen-year-olds is their *reading ability at the age of seven*. This has an effect on later achievement almost three times greater than other commonly investigated influences. Similar research carried out across the water in the USA in 1996 confirmed these findings.

Even if the early edge boys have over girls in visual-spatial abilities (see page 17) might eventually make some difference to their performance in subjects such as geometry or mechanical engineering, reading is the first gateway to all academic knowledge. And it is here that education systems are failing.

The reason boys are being turned off school is becoming obvious: right from the beginning they are not succeeding there. Quite simply, schools are not teaching them how to read. And reading ability does not merely affect academic achievement. Children who do not learn to read at an early stage are destined never to reach their full intellectual potential.

6 Learning to read

Parents make the reasonable assumption that children will learn how to read at school. These days, however, this is not a safe assumption to make. In a great many industrialized countries, a large proportion of children are failing to learn how to read, with wide-ranging consequences for their educational lives and beyond.

National testing of reading achievement in the United States reveals that more than half of children aged nine are unable to read fluently and appropriately for their age. In England, a third of children cannot read after having spent two years in school, and there are many schools where as many as 70 percent of eleven-year-olds are struggling with reading. By the time children are fifteen, only 7 percent of them manage to attain a grade C or better in English examinations. In Canada, more than half the thirteen-year-olds are currently unable to read without considerable difficulty.

A worldwide gender gap

Although neither boys nor girls are learning to read as well as they should, reading difficulties are far more common among boys.

Two international surveys of reading ability, known as the PISA 2000 and the PIRLS 2001 surveys – the first an Organization for Economic Cooperation and Development study and the second a study by the U.S. International Association for the Evaluation of Educational Achievement (IEA, for short) – highlight this gender gap. Together, these two surveys measured reading achievement in more than 50 countries. The results are disturbing. At ages nine and fifteen, the reading skills of boys are not just worse than girls', but are horrendously worse. And, for the first time in the history of such surveys, these very large gender differences in performance are occurring in virtually every country.

Not only are sex differences in reading showing up in more and more countries, but over the years the gender gap has been growing larger. Of the countries surveyed, 37 were also surveyed previously in 1991 in

26 out of 42 countries, and better than boys in one country – Albania. In science, girls scored as well as boys in most countries, and in two countries they scored significantly higher. One of these two countries was New Zealand, a country where the gender gap in reading ability at the age of nine is the largest among 33 countries surveyed.

Early success is crucial

Once a child starts school, probably the most stimulating experience to which his brain will be exposed is learning how to read. Early success not only has wide-ranging intellectual benefits, but brings social and emotional advantages as well. Studies show that early reading ability is highly predictive of a child's later self-concept and attitude toward school.

A rocky future

Being unable to read severely limits a child's experience in every school activity and area of study. And outside school, how narrow the world becomes when you are unable to read a train timetable, a menu, a newspaper, the instructions to a computer game or a list of emergency procedures. As boys grow older, the frustration that results from failing to learn how to read exacts a serious toll. In a study involving delinquent adolescent boys, the factor found to correlate most highly with aggression was reading failure.

Recent surveys in England show that boys are twice as likely as girls to be unhappy at school, fail to do their homework, misbehave in lessons or play truant.

In another study, reading disability in nine-year-old boys was found to predict juvenile delinquency at the age of fifteen. In a large U.S. government survey, a direct link between illiteracy and crime was demonstrated; it was found that more than 85 percent of minors entering the juvenile justice system could not read.

an earlier IEA study. In thirteen of these countries, sex differences that did not exist in 1991 were newly in evidence in 2001. In addition, from 1991 to 2001, the gap between the average reading scores for each sex widened in every country but one.

The link between early reading and academic achievement

Although young boys in England once read as well as girls, by the early 1980s, testing of seven-year-olds revealed that boys were significantly behind. The effect of this early underperformance in reading was brought home in the 1993 examination results for sixteen-year-olds: for the first time, girls outperformed boys, not just in English, but in every single subject.

A similar phenomenon is occurring in many other countries. Historically, boys have always tended to outperform girls in mathematics and science subjects. But now, with gender gaps in reading ability on the increase, girls are beginning not only to catch up, but also to overtake them in these subjects. In mathematics, the PISA survey revealed that fifteen-year-old girls' performance was equal to boys in

6 Boys' reading problems: causes and solutions

Boys' underachievement in reading is now a major problem. Educators and governments are desperately thrashing around trying to determine the cause and how to fix it. Many believe the way the male brain is structured and develops is at the root of the problem, and others point the finger at environmental factors. Here are some of the causes and solutions put forward – but are they the answer?

Is the male brain to blame?

CAUSES AND SOLUTIONS

Boys begin school with poorer verbal skills.
○ They should start school a year later than girls.

Boys are more curious and active, have short attention spans, and can't sit still.
○ They need to be put in single-sex classes and permitted to move around and talk more.

Boys' fine motor skills are poorer than girls', and printing and writing are difficult and unpleasant for them.
○ Delay their school start for a year; reduce the amount of written work or permit more use of computers.

Boys are more competitive, so find cooperative group learning less appealing.
○ Teach them in all-boy classes and introduce more competitions.

Boys, due to their testosterone levels and relative immaturity, are more aggressive, badly behaved and disruptive in class.
○ They should start school at a later age and, if necessary, be prescribed amphetamine-like drugs to calm them down.

DO THESE IDEAS MAKE SENSE?

First, it is clear that none of these perceptions about boys applies to all boys, or even the majority of boys. Boys seem to lag behind girls in their language skills only because, in the case of speech delays or problems, more boys are affected than girls (although see Q&A, page 133). Contrary to popular belief, boys are actually *better* than girls on some verbal tests, including tests of general knowledge, verbal reasoning and analogies.

Second, these supposed brain-related causes of boys' underachievement overlook the substantial impact of environmental influences, both at home *and at school*. These can affect a boy's language development, his ability to read, his fine motor skills, his concentration levels and whether he will be aggressive, become frustrated or behave badly.

Most important, although boys and girls do differ biologically, they always have! If such differences did not produce gender differences in reading in the past (see page 113), why ought we to consider them now?

Is the environment to blame?

CAUSES AND SOLUTIONS

Too many primary- or elementary-school teachers are female.
- ○ Hire more male teachers and involve fathers more in school life.

Boys are humiliated when girls read so much better.
- ○ Have single-sex schools, or single-sex classes, especially for English.

Boys no longer consider it "cool" to do well in reading, writing, spelling or, later, in English.
- ○ Invite into the school male role models (such as football or basketball players) who like to read.

With the advent of television and computer activities, boys find less time for leisure reading.
- ○ Teachers should make available reading material that will attract boys (comics, game instructions).

Dads are not reading enough to, or with, their sons.
- ○ Fathers and sons should read more together.

Reading tests requiring writing disadvantage boys, who do better on multiple-choice tests.
- ○ Increase objective testing and decrease subjective forms of measurement.

School starts when boys are too immature to cope.
- ○ Boys should start school one year later.

Teachers often have lower expectations of boys.
- ○ Eliminate bias by abolishing school entrance tests.

School practices fail to engage boys' right-hemisphere skills.
- ○ Vary teaching and testing strategies.

DO THESE IDEAS MAKE SENSE?

Most teachers of younger children are female (as they were in the past) and research consistently shows that the sex of a child's teacher has no impact on performance. Boys may become humiliated when girls "catch on" more quickly, but research shows that boys do not do better in single-sex schools – only girls do.

Inviting male role models into the classroom will not teach boys to read, however much they would like to succeed at it. It is like saying, "Oh look! Here's an exciting plane; if you *watch* this football player fly it, you will know how to fly it, too!" Encouraging boys to read by exposing them to material that might interest them is an excellent idea, but only for boys who *already* know how to read. They will not learn how to read this way any more than they will by listening to their father read to them. These strategies may help to pique boys' interest and boost their imaginations, vocabularies and thinking skills, but none will help them learn how to read.

A switch to more objective testing is unlikely to make the gender divide in reading disappear. The questions used in international surveys of reading ability *were* largely multiple-choice. The gender gap is real.

Starting school later, say at the age of seven, is not the answer. It does not work for boys in Norway, Finland and Sweden (see page 119).

The key to boosting teachers' expectations of boys is not to abolish tests, but to eradicate sex differences in reading.

Finally, that schools fail to engage boys' right-hemisphere skills is a curious accusation since current teaching methods encourage the development of right-hemisphere skills almost exclusively.

The real reason for boys' underachievement

None of the suggested causes – biological or environmental – provides an adequate explanation for boys' underperformance in reading. In the past, boys learned to read as well as girls, in spite of differences in their brains, language abilities or fine motor skills. In fact, many boys even now, despite the lure of computer games and television, are learning to read as well as, *if not better than*, girls.

But boys who are learning to read successfully are being taught to read by a certain method of instruction. These boys perform just as well as girls regardless of their teacher's sex, their school starting

age, the kinds of reading tests they take or any of the other biological and environmental factors that might come into play.

Any teacher who uses this particular method not only immediately (if inadvertently) eradicates sex differences, but also produces significantly better reading attainment among both boys *and* girls than with the use of other approaches. Indeed, teachers using this method are convinced that the steady move away from this form of teaching over the last 30 years is *the* cause of the new gender divide in reading ability.

Before exploring teaching methods further, let us consider briefly exactly what reading involves.

What is reading?

If you have been told that learning to read, or even teaching a child to read, is a tricky and complex process, it's time to jettison that idea. Learning to read is easy. It does have to be taught, but all children can be taught to read. In fact, research shows that children with an IQ as low as 50 can be taught to read.

We don't even have to guess any more about how best to teach a child to read. By combining the evidence from eye movement studies and brain-scans, we now know that reading consists of four steps:

- **Letter shape recognition** – eyes focus on each letter in turn, analyzing the shapes and recognizing them one by one, from left to right
- **Letter-to-sound translation** – each recognized letter is translated into a sound; the child remembers that, for example, the shape "s" stands for the sound "ssss"
- **Sound blending** – each sound is blended with the next one, until the sound of the whole word emerges
- **Meaning retrieval** – the "sound" of the word triggers the retrieval of its meaning.

By the age of ten all this begins to happen quickly. Letter groups seen millions of times (such as *ing, ed, ee, str, er*) are no longer translated letter by letter into sound. The brain begins to recognize familiar letter chunks and translates them immediately into sound.

So, a child must remember two sets of information:
- what different letter shapes look like
- what sound each letter shape "says" or stands for

and learn two techniques:

Playing letter-sound games

You can give your son an absolutely amazing head start with reading if you teach him, not letter names, but letter sounds. Your son will love learning these if you devise games that involve lots of movement or finding a target. Use an alphabet frieze to play these games.

Alphabet trip

Have your son run to locate different pictures (representing the letters) randomly as you name them. Later, see how far he can "travel," naming all the pictures in order from the beginning (apple, bee, cake…). Praise him for his cleverness.

Talking letters

Point to the letter "s" and say, "This squiggle tells you what sound the picture starts with." Say "ssss" and have him imitate you. Then: "Can you hear 'ssss' at the beginning of sssnake [or whatever else is pictured]? What does it say again?" Give him hugs and praise him highly.

Teach other lowercase letters in the same way and then play a game by randomly pointing to the letters he knows and asking him to make them "talk" by saying their sound. When he knows ten letter sounds well, move on to this version of the game: "I can hear a letter talking – ssss, ssss, ssss! Where is it? Can you find it? Run and cover it up to make it stop talking!"

- how to sound out a word from left to right
- how to blend the letter sounds in a word together.

Pre-reading alphabet knowledge is *the* most important determinant of reading achievement. The key, however, is to remember that it is a particular kind of alphabet knowledge that will make all the difference – letter sounds.

6 How could teaching methods be to blame?

Teaching methods are rarely named in speculating about the causes of boys' underachievement. After all, how could a single factor be the culprit, when most teachers will tell you that they use not one but a variety of different strategies? Read on to find out whether the style your son's teacher uses is the reason for his lack of reading success.

Essentially, there are two kinds of beginning reading instruction: the popular multi-focus method and the single-focus method.

The multi-focus approach

This approach involves children in a wide variety of activities thought to be helpful when learning how to read. Often referred to as *eclectic, whole-language, a mix of methods, balanced,* or *no one method*, it usually includes some or all of the following:

○ memorization of a large number of words based on their appearance

○ memorization of entire texts via repetitive shared reading and guessing at words using context or pictures

○ phonological awareness (that is, where children are taught to detect the rhyming sounds, or in the case of phoneme awareness letter sounds, in spoken words)

○ phonics (occasional attention to letter names or letter sounds while reading, usually only to the first letter of a word)

○ analytic phonics (guessing what sound the initial, final or medial letter in a word stands for or what sound a letter chunk makes after hearing the teacher pronounce a word or words shown in print).

The single-focus approach

This method concentrates on the explicit teaching of the two sets of *initial* processes that must be mastered in order to read: the two sets of knowledge (letter

shapes and letter sounds) and the two skills (sounding out and blending) (see page 117). It is often known as the *phonics* approach. But, beware! The term "phonics" is often applied to methods that do not remotely resemble what is being described here.

What research tells us

A large body of reliable research consistently demonstrates that the more a method is focused on the direct teaching of the two sets of information and the two skills used during reading, the faster and better children learn to read. The more time a teacher spends on teaching other things, the slower and the lower the reading achievement.

Large classrooms studies in Scotland, Canada, England and the USA that have compared the effects of different teaching methods are particularly convincing: they show that single-focus-taught children end up with reading ages as much as one to two years above their actual ages, whereas those taught by other methods can often wind up reading or spelling *well below* their age level.

In a large classroom study in Canada, conducted by Karen Sumbler and Dale Willows in 1996, it was found that time spent engaged in the following six activities makes *no difference* to beginners' reading achievement:

- phonological awareness training
- sight word learning (memorizing words)
- shared reading
- class chanting of patterned or rhyming books
- any attempt to write text
- the learning of letter names

Sex differences are eradicated by the single-focus method, and sometimes boys even outperform girls. For example, Scottish research examined the long-term effects of this form of instruction. Five years on, boys taught by the single-focus method were reading at a level not only two and a half years above their age but also seven months *ahead* of similarly taught girls.

Did you know...?
The most dramatic sex differences in reading in the world are occurring in countries where multi-focus methods are the norm – New Zealand, Singapore, Finland, Norway, Sweden, Australia, Switzerland, Australia, England, Canada and the United States. New Zealand's nine-year-olds display a gender gap equaled only by that found in Belize – the country that scored lowest in the world.

British government surveys confirm these results. In England, multi-focus methods swept into use in the late 1960s and early 1970s, but infiltrated Scottish schools much later. After the introduction of these methods in England, it was discovered that the average English child was reading at a level *18 months below* that of the average Scottish child. During this same period, significant sex differences in reading began to appear. These were apparent by the late 1970s and early 1980s in England, but did not appear in Scotland until the late 1990s.

Why are educators attracted to multi-focus methods?

It's easy to see why these methods, which began in the United States and then spread around the world, have become so popular. The multi-focus approach is well-intentioned, motivated by a desire to meet the needs of all pupils. Unfortunately, it carries one danger – it's easy for teachers to lose sight of how much time they are spending on what. As an example: I conducted a detailed time-sampling analysis of a nationwide reading program designed to help end-of-first-year failing readers. The results were hair-raising: the amount of lesson time allocated to activities that actually had an effect on and did improve reading ability was just 3 percent.

Why certain methods disadvantage boys

Of course, there was never any intention to disadvantage boys. But it turns out that the multi-focus approach has a propensity to dwell on the very practices that just happen to be bad for boys or, more specifically, particularly bad for the young, developing male brain. By contrast, the single-focus approach just happens to circumvent the brain differences between sexes that have the potential to cause problems for boys when learning to read. In short, the multi-focus method gives boys exactly what they don't need, and the single-focus method gives them precisely what they do. There are at least six reasons for this.

1 Boys have a brain that specializes

When reading, boys' brains are primarily active in left-hemisphere regions, whereas girls' brain activity is more bilateral. Multi-method practices, however, fail to help boys develop the necessary left-hemisphere neural circuits because instruction focuses on activities that primarily engage boys' right hemispheres. Recent brain-imaging studies reveal that children taught by these methods actually develop patterns of brain activity that resemble those of dyslexics – that is, mostly right-hemisphere sites are active (see page 133).

2 Boys have a different timetable of brain development

Because the male brain favors right-hemisphere development over left during the early years, reading instruction directed at boys needs to stimulate their brains to shift their focus to the left hemisphere. Also, because neural connections between the two halves of the brain grow more slowly in boys, the method of reading instruction should encourage the dominant right hemisphere to grow connections to the left.

TEACHING PRACTICES AND THE BRAIN HEMISPHERES ACTIVATED BY THEM IN BOYS

Single-focus practices		Multi-focus practices	
letter-to-sound translation: recognize a letter shape … and translate to sound	RH to LH	phonological awareness: detect sound in a word … and then associate with a letter	LH to RH
sound out letters in a word	LH	pictures used to guess at words	RH
blend the sounds of a word	LH	memorize words based on shape	RH

The box above shows how single-focus methods do both these things in contrast to multi-focus methods.

3 Boys find left- to right-hemisphere tasks harder

Stanford University research demonstrated in 1983 that boys have significantly more trouble than girls translating a sound (a left-hemisphere task) into a letter shape (a right-hemisphere task). But in recognizing letters (a right-hemisphere task) and translating into sound (a left-hemisphere task), the sexes perform equally.

This means that boys are disadvantaged by methods that involve deducing sound-to-letter relationships (analytic phonics). For boys, attending to letters *first* is simply an easier and more natural task for them (because their right-hemisphere skills are stronger) than having to attend to *speech sounds* first.

4 Boys tend to have less pre-school alphabet knowledge than girls

Most children know a number of letters by name before they begin school, but very few children know some letter sounds. Studies show that those who do tend to be girls. Boys will therefore be disadvantaged in multi-methods classrooms where letter-to-sound instruction is minimal or non-existent. Single-focus instruction helps boys to catch up quickly in this fundamentally important area.

5 Young boys have weaker visual memories than girls

In 1999, a team of researchers headed by Anne Soderman conducted a large study, involving the USA, Taiwan and India, that measured, among other things, the visual memory abilities of children aged six to eight. Boys were found to have significantly poorer visual memory abilities. Other research confirms this sex difference. Unlike the multi-focus method, single-focus teaching does not rely on good visual memory. Instead of having to memorize huge numbers of words based on their visual appearance, children translate each letter in a word one by one into sound. And since memory for sounds does not differ between the sexes, there is no discrimination against boys.

6 Boys have poorer print-tracking abilities

The Soderman study also revealed that boys are not quite as good as girls of the same age in their ability to track print across a page without losing their place. In multi-focus classrooms the left-to-right tracking of a line of print (a left-hemisphere task) is disrupted when attention is drawn to pictures, words, shapes or initial letters of words (which are all right-hemisphere tasks).

In single-focus classrooms, reading lines of text is introduced later. Children first learn to read words in isolation. During the systematic, sequential left-to-right sounding out of letters in words, children's eyes are trained to track print in the correct way.

6 Logical and creative thinking

Society may regard males as the more logical sex and females as the more intuitive, but is this a popular misconception or is it true? And if it is true, does this affect how girls and boys approach different school subjects and how well they do in them?

IQ tests furnish both verbal scores, an indication of left-hemisphere, logical thinking abilities, and non-verbal scores, an indication of right-hemisphere, intuitive thinking abilities. But because intelligence tests have been explicitly designed to minimize sex differences they cannot be used to answer the question of whether there is a true difference between the sexes in these forms of intelligence.

Evidence from other tests points to a slight female advantage on verbal tests and a male advantage on non-verbal ones. Age may make the difference, though, in whether girls or boys show a preference for one type of thinking or the other. To what extent, for instance, might the course of boys' and girls' brain development affect their thinking styles?

Left = analytical; right = intuitive

Generally speaking, it is the right side of the brain that is the intuitive and creative side, whereas the left is the logical, analytical side. The thinking approach of the right hemisphere is holistic: it perceives things simultaneously. The left hemisphere, on the other hand, is sequential in its approach: thinking is step by step, and things are perceived one at a time.

You can see this division of brain labor reflected in how young boys and girls play. During the early years, when boys' brains are concentrating on right-brain development, their play often involves fantasy figures and original scenarios. By contrast, girls, whose brains favor left-hemisphere growth at this time, like to take on the roles of real people and act out real-life events and routines.

Changing gear

During the first years in school, boys' brains have developed fewer brain connections in the frontal region (see page 70). As a result, they may find it more difficult to apply themselves and attend to their work. But, when boys' left-hemisphere development begins to take off, between six and eleven, it continues until about sixteen, whereas the later, less dramatic shift of girls' brains to right-hemisphere development happens over a shorter period, about five years or so. As the parts of boys' brains implicated in non-verbal calculations and spatial skills (in the right hemisphere) and mathematical reasoning (in the left hemisphere) begin to grow ever more connections, their efficiency accelerates at this time in comparison to girls. These different patterns of development may help to explain sex differences in performance in mathematics at different ages. For more, see page 127.

Later, under normal circumstances about age six or seven, a shift toward increasing growth of left-hemisphere neural networks occurs in boys. The opposite shift (to increased growth in the right hemisphere) occurs in girls, but in their case not until the age of eight or nine. And since girls' brains operate in a less one-sided fashion, this shift is less dramatic. In terms of brain growth, boys' right-hemisphere development and girls' left-hemisphere development receives less attention in favor of the opposite hemisphere at these ages.

Teaching that promotes creativity and logical thinking skills

Although the hemispheres are specialized in function to some extent, there is constant interplay between the two (see page 14). For any particular task, the brain will choose to activate myriad brain sites, usually the most appropriate ones for the job. However, these patterns of activation are established as a result of experience and training.

Since much of this training takes place in the classroom, the choice of teaching method is particularly important for boys. Their later development of the frontal brain region (in charge of attending, and monitoring and controlling behavior) means that for all school subjects, boys will respond best to direct, explicit teaching.

Boys have an innate desire to get a grip on how things work (see page 130) – and quickly. Deductive teaching methods can slow the pace of learning and lead to frustration in boys. Furthermore, real creativity and originality (which can play a part in almost every endeavor) cannot blossom in a knowledge vacuum. Children of both sexes who are no longer taught times tables or letter-sound associations in case it dampens their creativity are denied the fundamental skills and knowledge needed to fulfill their intellectual potential.

Boys' natural talents

It has been found that females excel on tests that measure visual matching, fine motor skills and verbal fluency, and males excel on tests measuring visual targeting, mental rotation, and mathematical reasoning. These gender differences in cognitive strengths perfectly reflect the differences in how boys' and girls' brains grow. Boys, whose brains concentrate on right-hemisphere growth to begin with, and girls, whose brains do the opposite, tend to be better at the various abilities that emerge the earliest.

Generally speaking, however, ability differences between the sexes (with the exception of mental rotation and visual targeting skills: see page 100) are not huge. A far more striking phenomenon is the substantially wider range of ability scores that occur among boys. This means that, whatever the ability, there will be many more boys than girls scoring at the very top of the scale and at the very low end. As a result, not only are many more boys than girls identified as "learning disabled," but there are also many more boys identified as "gifted."

Special talents of boys

Boys can aim at and strike a target more accurately. They are better at intercepting moving objects, such as catching a ball.

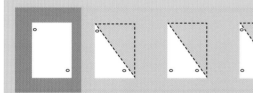

From a young age, boys tend to perform better than girls on some spatial tasks. They do well on tests like this that involve mentally rotating simple shapes

or determining where the punched holes in a sheet of paper will fall when it is folded in half.

500	If only 80% of eggs hatch, how many eggs must the farmer start out with to ensure there will be 400 chickens?

Boys also do better than girls on tests that measure mathematical reasoning.

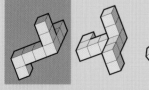

And they can remember better whether a 3-D object is the same as one seen previously.

Special talents of girls

Girls tend to perform better on tests of perceptual speed, such as rapidly identifying matching items.

 sea, snow, sleep, snail, stop, sail, sad, sand, soap, sip, sap, soup, silly, seek, seal, sale...

Girls are better than boys at naming as many words as possible that start with a given letter within a limited time

and they do better on fine motor tasks that require precision movement and fast coordination, such as quickly placing pegs in holes.

95	$17 \times 4 - 9 + 36 = ?$
70	$3(12 + 9) + 11 - \dfrac{16}{4} = ?$

Also, girls are slightly better at straightforward arithmetic.

Girls can better remember whether an object or a number of objects has been displaced.

6 Mathematics: a male forte?

Research shows that among children with extremely high mathematical ability, boys outnumber girls by as much as thirteen to one. But among average students, even though boys tend to outscore girls, the magnitude of their differences is small. Data also suggests that girls tend to be better than boys in straightforward arithmetic; boys are better at mathematical reasoning and geometry; and girls often outperform boys during the early years but boys generally outdo them later on (see Changing gear, page 123)

This picture of mathematics could be changing, though. In 1995, the mathematics achievement of final year secondary pupils was measured in 24 countries (known as the TIMMS survey). Boys outperformed girls in every country by a significant margin. A few years later, the PISA 2000 survey measured fifteen-year-olds' mathematics performance. Strictly speaking, a direct comparison of results cannot be made, but this data does suggest that girls have been catching up. In the later survey, while boys outperformed girls in fifteen countries, girls scored as well as boys in 26 countries and even outscored them in one country. But why are there these apparent sex differences? Is it environment or biology?

A true story...

At the age of two, Joshua Bright knew his two, three and ten times tables. At the age of five, he busies himself working on algebra, geometry and square roots, in preparation for an examination in a few months' time. The exam? It's the high school examination in mathematics for fifteen-year-olds. Although his parents encouraged his interest by involving him in mathematical games or activities both before and after school, they are amazed at their son's abilities. They do not regard themselves as pushy parents. For Joshua, mathematics is what he enjoys most. It's his favorite form of play.

Mathematics and society's expectations

Two environmental influences – societal attitudes and sex differences in leisure-time activities – are likely to feature in how well boys and girls perform in mathematics. Attitudes are changing, but if a girl believes she won't do well on a test, her score will reflect that. In one study, girls scored below boys on a mathematics test, but when specifically told the test was unbiased to either gender, they scored just as well as the boys.

Young boys are given, and like to play with, toys that develop visual-spatial skills – blocks, construction sets, model planes. Later, these skills are further

scores. During childhood, testosterone levels do not differ between the sexes, but could the surge in boys' testosterone levels during the first six months of life and, later, as puberty approaches contribute to their slight edge over girls? The early surge is likely to contribute to boys' preference for certain toys and computer games, and the later rise could explain why, if boys do outperform girls in mathematics classes, it is usually later in school life (see page 123).

Testosterone may lead to brain changes that lend boys a further advantage. The region thought to be involved in mathematical processing is called the temporal-parietal area. Within this area in each hemisphere is a structure called the inferior parietal lobule or IPL for short. After correcting for males' larger brain size, the IPL has been found to be 6 percent larger overall in the brains of adult males compared with females. Furthermore, whereas in female brains the right IPL is slightly larger, in males the left side is noticeably larger; this structure was found to be especially large in the brain of Albert Einstein.

So, a question arises: Does experience contribute to its larger size in males or is this the way the IPL is *programmed* to develop? Or, could there be an interaction between these two factors, leading to boys' apparent edge in mathematics?

Scientists are still trying to pin down exactly what happens in the brains of males and females when they tackle various kinds of mathematical problems. So far, the evidence suggests that, for males at least, areas within the temporal-parietal region are activated bilaterally, but are more pronounced on one side of the brain or the other, depending on the type of task.

honed via computer or video games. In one survey, boys aged eight to fourteen were found to spend more than twice as much time as girls playing computer games. In a study of 2,200 eight- and nine-year-olds, computer games were the most popular leisure-time activity among boys – a third of boys played on a regular basis, compared with only a tenth of girls.

Mathematics and biological sex differences

Hormonal and brain differences may also contribute to gender differences in performance. Males with testosterone levels in the low to normal range are found to do the best in spatial tests, and very high testosterone levels are associated with a decline in spatial scores. Very high levels of testosterone in females, however, are linked with high spatial test

The power of music

Because boys are slower to develop connections between the two halves of the brain and appear to develop fewer of them than girls, something that encourages this development might be especially beneficial to boys. And it seems that there is something that does just that – music.

Just listening to music engages the entire brain, synchronizing brain waves and making the brain operate more efficiently. This is why it is much easier to learn abstract information (such as the letters of the alphabet, or the number of days in each month) if it is put to music or rhyme.

Learning to play a musical instrument may be particularly beneficial. Research shows that among musicians *who started their training in early childhood*, the corpus callosum or central connector between the hemispheres (see page 18) is up to 15 percent larger than in people with little or no musical training.

Something special about playing an instrument...?

Instruction was given to two groups of seven-year-olds; each group spent time playing computer games involving geometric puzzles and mentally manipulating shapes, but additionally, while one group was taught extra English, the other received piano keyboard lessons. After four months, the researchers discovered that the additional keyboard lessons had produced a startling difference. Children in this group scored 27 percent higher than the other group in proportions and fractions tests.

Studies show that, as well as aiding mathematical proficiency, musical training can enhance language ability. The brain's speech perception area (which, by the way, contains that mathematics-related structure, the IPL [see page 127]) is already larger on the left side in boys' brains compared with girls', and one study discovered that it is even larger in musicians – in some cases, more than 130 percent larger!

It appears that this area is responsible not only for categorizing speech sounds, but also categorizing musical sounds. This helps to explain why other studies have found that musical training can accelerate language skills.

Another true story...

A gifted boy, Sho Yano became at age twelve the youngest trainee doctor in the world. He has an IQ of 200. Like many child prodigies, he is extremely musical and regards mathematics as child's play. His mother noticed his special musical gifts when, at the age of three, he was able to copy a Chopin melody that she had been playing on the piano. At four, he began composing pieces of music for his family.

Did you know...?

Chess speeds brain development. As when listening to music, many regions of the brain are engaged during the playing of chess. So this kind of stimulation may also speed up the growth of interhemispheric connections in boys' brains. Findings reveal that, for both boys and girls, regular chess playing can

○ raise IQ,

○ boost memory and verbal reasoning abilities,

○ enhance problem-solving ability and critical thinking,

○ produce superior reading achievement,

○ increase the ability to concentrate,

○ enhance originality and creativity,

○ result in higher English and mathematics scores,

○ raise confidence and self-esteem.

Chess is an especially good game for boys. It appeals to their desire to compete; they can establish their prowess in an area where they are naturally inclined to excel. If he doesn't already have one, you may wish to invest in a chess set for your son.

6 A scientific frame of mind

To some parents, it may seem that boys are the natural scientists, conducting an endless series of experiments. How many toys can fit in the washing machine? What happens when red paint gets flushed down the toilet? What can be inside this clock? Is it that boys are more destructive than girls or is their mania for conducting "experiments" simply because they are more inquisitive?

A University of Bristol study helps to answer this question. Young children aged two and a half to three years old were presented with a task to test whether they understood object permanence. The toddlers watched as an object rolled behind a screen from which a solid wall protruded at the top. Visually, it looked as though the object was impossible to retrieve. Both boys and girls spent longer looking at this "impossible" outcome than when the protruding wall was absent. But, when the toddlers were told they could search for the object, a fascinating difference emerged. Far more boys than girls made successful forays to retrieve the object.

This experiment illustrates boys' "hunter instincts" driven by their amygdalas or "tigers" (see page 18) at work. The boys were more adventurous and curious about something that appeared to be quite inexplicable. Their need to conquer (greater than girls because of their larger "tigers") spurred them on to solve this challenging object-in-space problem.

But it is important to keep in mind that girls are intrigued with a different aspect of their environment. It is likely that curiosity strikes boys and girls in pretty equal measure. It is just that they are curious about different things – boys may be more curious about how *things* operate, whereas girls may be more interested in how *people* operate.

Under the microscope

International TIMMS surveys reveal that thirteen-year-old girls' science scores increased significantly over the years from 1995 to 1999, while boys' average scores remained the same. In the PISA 2000 survey of fifteen-year-olds' science abilities, in all but nine of 42 countries, no sex differences were apparent. In six countries, girls outperformed boys, and in three others boys did better.

Other research indicates that boys generally outperform girls in physics and chemistry on standardized tests given at the ages of thirteen and fifteen, but that the sexes achieve equally in biology. To put things in perspective, though, any differences between boys and girls in their science performance is minute in comparison to the differences that exist within each gender group. And, as in mathematics, more boys than girls are found at the extreme ends of any score distributions.

Parental attitudes

Researchers at the University of California wondered, when gender differences in science test performance are not large, why so few females pursued scientific or science-based careers.

After studying adolescents and their families while they conducted science or non-science tasks, their findings revealed that parents were more likely to believe that science was less interesting and more difficult for daughters than for sons. Parents' beliefs influenced how interested in and how self-confident children were about science, and fathers tended to use more complex speech with sons than with daughters during scientific tasks.

Although more and more women are succeeding in scientific careers, societal attitudes are still stacked against them. Women constitute fewer than one-quarter of the scientists in the United States, a state of affairs mirrored in Europe.

6 School-related problems

Most children have problems at school at some stage of their educational lives. So, here is some practical advice so that you can be prepared, along with further information on the topics in this chapter.

Q How can I tell if my son is being bullied at school and what can I do about it?

A Children who fail in the classroom may seek to bolster their wounded ego by lording it over others physically or verbally in the playground. Both reading problems and school bullying are on the rise, especially among boys. In England, 60 percent of secondary pupils (the majority boys) worry about being bullied by other children.

What you can do

○ Be alert for the following signs: a sudden fear of walking to school, truanting, decline in academic performance, sudden withdrawn behavior or a refusal to tell you what's wrong.

○ Talk to the head teacher or principal; discuss the school's policy on bullying and what can be done.

○ Rather than asking your son what's wrong, ask him directly if he is being teased or bullied.

○ Arrange for your son to get tips on how to handle bullying. A school counselor or an older boy can show him how to behave more assertively. Martial arts training can increase confidence.

Q If delaying school stunts a child's IQ, does early schooling make children more intelligent?

A Evidence suggests that children from disadvantaged backgrounds can benefit tremendously both socially and intellectually from pre-school programs, and to some extent, other children can, too. Parents must choose carefully, however, since the *quality* of the school makes a tremendous difference.

Q Our son is reaching the end of his first year at school. We're worried that he is not learning how to read properly. His teacher says his reading is average and there is no need to worry. What should we do?

A By this stage, your son should be a good reader. (Children taught by the single-focus method learn to read after sixteen weeks.) Don't be put off by reassurances that boys are just slower to catch on, or eventually catch up.

If you do not have access to someone who knows how to teach reading in the single-focus way (see page 118), the safest and quickest course is to take matters into your own hands. Don't worry! This is not as daunting as it may sound and you don't need any special training. Teach your son what letters and letter combinations stand for which sounds by playing letter-sound games (see page 117) until his letter-to-sound decoding becomes fast and fluent. Have fun; devise active games. Teach him to sound out magnetic letters and blend sounds together to read simple words.

Q Our son spends several hours a day playing computer games. Should we be worried?

A While frequent computer or video game playing has been shown to improve hand-eye coordination, reaction time, emotional state, visual-spatial skills, creative thinking, problem-solving and mathematics abilities, some studies find negative effects. Moderation is the key; restrict computer-based sessions to allow your son time for exercise and homework.

Q Isn't dyslexia an inherited brain disorder? And why are so many more boys than girls affected?

A Yale neuroscientists discovered that schools identify four times more boys than girls as dyslexic. But when researchers actually screened for dyslexia, they found equal numbers of boys and girls affected. They concluded that, perhaps because girls are behaviorally less troublesome, dyslexia in girls is routinely underdiagnosed. Although it is commonly believed that children can inherit a built-in predisposition to developing reading problems, no evidence that dyslexia is X-linked (affecting more boys; see page 82) has ever been reported.

There is, however, considerable evidence that environmental factors ranging from autoimmune disorders in the womb to birth trauma, chronic ear infections or certain teaching methods can play a role. In 2002, University of Texas researchers showed how a particular type of instruction can "cure" dyslexia. They gave dyslexics (mostly boys) aged seven to seventeen 80 hours of single-focus reading instruction. They scanned their brains before and afterward. Before the training when they were reading, their brains were operating like the classic dyslexic – mainly lighting up on the right side. After the training, the scientists were astonished to discover that their brain patterns had become just like those of normal male readers (mostly lighting up in areas on the *left*).

7 making a man

7 Shaping a boy's personality

Mary and Stephen are taking a weekend break, a four-hour car journey from home. They have left behind their sixteen-year-old son, Adam, and have agreed that he can have friends over, perhaps for pizza. Later they phone to say good night. The telephone rings. And rings. And rings. More than an hour later, there is still no answer and they are starting to worry. Finally, Mary resolves to call a neighbor. Then they learn that a massive party is under way at their house – throngs of raucous young people, loud rock music, lawns decorated with empty bottles and beer cans, and wafts of softly scented smoke of suspicious origin.

It was inevitable. Eventually, all boys want the rest of the world to see that they are separate young men, no longer dependent on their parents. By the time a boy

reaches adolescence, he probably recognizes and appreciates the many positive aspects of his parents' personalities, but he has also begun to notice a few flaws. But he is different, and what better way to illustrate his individuality than by doing something that his parents would never allow him to do? The bonus is that it impresses his friends and his status goes up a notch or two. And among his peers, everyone knows what the rule is: "'When the parents are away, there's a place for us to play!'"

What kind of man will your son become?

We all want our sons to grow up to be happy, clever, responsible, successful, well-adjusted men. By attending to your son's physical and emotional needs, and by exposing him to varied and stimulating intellectual experiences, you can make a tremendous difference in his future.

But what is it that shapes a boy's personality, that molds him into the sort of man you want him to become? Most parents would not disagree that ideally

they'd like their son to become a person who is honest, funny, kind, gentle, loving, respectful, self-confident and, if at all possible, disinclined to follow, with the accuracy of a laser beam, the rules of his peers. Is there anything they can do to arrange it?

Temperament and personality

Some aspects of personality are actually innate. All parents, especially those with more than one child, know that babies, regardless of their sex, can differ enormously in their emotional and their social behavior. One baby is easygoing and adaptable, whereas the other is fussy and irritable. Another baby may be outgoing and uninhibited while the other is timid and shy. These inborn social and emotional traits refer to a child's temperament.

In Chapter 3 we saw that biological differences between boys and girls result in observable differences, right from birth, in their social and emotional behavior. Baby boys tend to respond less to social stimuli (human faces and voices) and make less eye contact than girls do, and their different brain structure also means that boys are inclined to behave more aggressively than girls.

You cannot do much about most aspects of temperament, but temperament is not the only factor that determines personality. In fact, personality is shaped much more by an individual's life experiences and, in particular, by the values and personalities of the people closest to him. The way a boy's mother, father, siblings and peers behave and interact with him will have a substantial influence on the kind of person he becomes and on the sort of relationships he forms with other people.

7 The importance of early attachment

Some people may think that the kind of care and attention you give a baby in the first year or two won't have serious ramifications in the long term. But this time seems to be incredibly important. Although the quality of the first attachment in infancy does not predict the total behavior of a person, the primary caregiver is likely to have a more powerful influence on a child's development than anyone else. This person is usually the mother.

The positive emotional connection that develops between a mother and her baby son is the first and most important influence on shaping a boy's personality. Indeed, psychologists consider early infant attachment to the primary caregiver to be the single, most critical event in shaping *any* child's personality.

A caregiver who is reliably available and responsive to a baby's needs forms the basis for competence in exploring the environment, forming other relationships and developing self-esteem.

Three patterns of attachment

Mary Ainsworth, a researcher working in this field in the 1960s, developed a way to classify and measure the nature of a child's first attachment by closely observing how babies of either sex behave when left with a stranger.

As a result of her research, she described two categories of attachment – secure or anxious. Furthermore, those babies who are anxiously attached to their primary caregiver come in two flavors – avoidant or ambivalent.

Secure

Securely attached babies use their mothers (or other attachment figures) as a safe emotional base from which to explore the world. They are at ease as long as they can see her. These babies, when moderately stressed by a brief three-minute separation, are visibly pleased to see Mother when she returns, go to her, seek comfort and reassurance, and with no open or masked anger, soon return to their exploration or play.

Anxious/*avoidant*

These babies are anxious and angry about their mothers' responsiveness and have developed a coping strategy. When the mother returns after the same sort of stressful event as described above, avoidant babies behave in a detached manner, fail to greet their mothers, ignore her overtures and act as if she is of little or no importance to them.

Anxious/*ambivalent*

In babies with ambivalent attachments, both positive and negative behavior toward the mother is readily observable. When reunited after brief separations in an unfamiliar environment, an anxious/ambivalent baby may simultaneously seek contact with his mother but also kick or hit her.

What are the outcomes of a baby's early attachment?

The way in which you treat your baby boy from day one can have wide-ranging influences on the sort of man he will become. If you invest the time in his first two years creating as secure an attachment as possible, it will pay off down the line – for both of you.

Securely attached children

If a child's early attachment is of the secure variety, his or her personality as a toddler and pre-schooler will be affected in a number of positive ways. Children who are securely attached to their mothers in infancy tend to be more persistent and enthusiastic in pursuing a task. Not only is their intellectual development accelerated, but their social and emotional development is further advanced compared with children who are insecurely attached. These children are found to be more cooperative, sociable, competent and "ego-resilient."

As adolescents and adults, those with secure patterns of attachment describe their most important love experiences as especially happy, friendly and trusting. Their relationships are found to last longer than those of their anxiously attached peers. Being securely

Early infant attachment...

○ is at the heart of normal brain development and healthy personality development;

○ lays the foundation for relating intimately with others, including spouses and children;

○ affects parents' abilities to nurture and to be responsive to their children;

○ is long-lasting and substantial in its effect, influencing generations of families.

attached even seems to be associated with a more effective, self-confident approach to work and greater career success.

7

Anxiously attached children

Children with these kinds of attachment do not generally develop psychiatric disorders, but they may be at greater risk for less than optimal brain development. Evidence shows that elevated stress hormones can be hazardous to the brain (see page 59). Babies judged to be anxiously attached to their mothers show higher stress hormone levels in response to strange or fearful events than babies judged to be securely attached, and this at a time when brain growth is normally at its peak.

Anxious/avoidant children's behavior is characterized by detachment, hiding their feelings and difficulty in recognizing and expressing emotions. Invariably, they do not ask for help or emotional support, lacking trust that people around them will respond positively. In terms of their play time, they mostly play with objects, engage in only a limited amount of fantasy play and have trouble acknowledging their own mistakes.

As adolescents and adults they have difficulty building and maintaining intimate relationships. They are described as "distant," often have few close friends, and fear and jealousy may be a feature of their relationships. Often compulsive about their work, they also tend to idealize their parents.

Anxious/ambivalent children are often less persistent, enthusiastic and compliant than those classified as secure. They tend to express more anger and frustration, often becoming bullies or victims during interactions with their peers. As adolescents or adults, they report love relationships that involve obsession, overwhelming jealousy, unrealistic demands, extreme sexual attraction, much self-doubt, lack of confidence and anxiety that others do not understand or appreciate them enough.

What determines how securely a child is attached?

Research shows that what principally determines attachment is how sensitive a mother is to her baby's needs. Mothers who are autonomous, nurturing and adaptable tend to have securely attached babies. Studies in the USA and Europe indicate that rejection, particularly ignoring a baby's bids for contact, lead to avoidant babies. Inconsistency and unpredictability – ignoring some of the time, intrusive at other times, and sometimes sensitive – result in a baby who is ambivalently attached.

Certain factors increase the risk of a baby being insecurely attached: depression or other psychiatric illness in the mother, circumstances where the mother lacks practical and emotional support, poor marital quality, extreme poverty and infant irritability. This last factor may account for the fact that some studies find that boys are more at risk for experiencing insecure patterns of attachment.

Are boys and girls equally likely to be securely attached?

Hundreds of studies involving infants, toddlers and pre-schoolers have reported no sex differences in the incidence of insecure attachment or in the effect of different attachment patterns in adolescence or adulthood. On the other hand, quite a number of studies have found that boys *are* more vulnerable than girls to insecure attachment or the consequences of it.

Although baby girls may be more responsive socially, baby boys may be the more sensitive sex. Newborn boys tend to be fussier, startle more easily and may be more difficult to console. The greater emotional demands they may make on their mothers may help to explain some of the research finding sex differences in attachment patterns.

In 1991, the U.S. National Institute of Child Health and Human Development, alarmed that studies were showing as many as 37 percent of children to be insecurely attached, decided to investigate the effects of early non-maternal child care. They found that boys and girls do not fare equally well. The social-emotional development of boys is more likely to suffer when their mothers are employed during their first year. However, analyzing a large number of studies, researchers concluded that more than half (55 percent) of babies whose mothers return to work when they are less than six months old are securely attached, versus almost two-thirds (65 percent) among non-working mothers. These figures do suggest a high proportion are not securely attached, but may include very young babies not yet attached but whose potential for secure attachment may not be under threat.

Researchers examined the effects on children's attachments when their mothers returned to work before they were six months old. They assessed mother-child and father-child attachment behavior when the babies were twelve months old. A trend was revealed suggesting that, in employed-mother families, boys were more likely to be insecurely attached to both their mothers and their fathers compared with girls whose mothers were employed, or to babies of either sex whose mothers were not employed. But, this was only a trend. There was stronger evidence that boys whose mothers were employed had significantly less secure attachments to their *fathers*.

Temperament and attachment

In a study of the influences of infant temperament, maternal sensitivity and gender were investigated. Internationally adopted children, who were placed with families before six months of age, were followed from infancy to the age of seven. Results showed that girls were better adjusted than boys, except in intellectual development. Easy temperament in an infant was found to be later associated with higher levels of social, cognitive and personality development and fewer behavioral problems. This finding suggests that, in this group of children at least, more males than females had difficult temperaments.

7 Are boys more vulnerable?

Research shows that males' physiological responses to emotion are much stronger than females'. They perspire more, their hearts beat faster and their brains trigger the release of more stress hormones. It may surprise you to know that in physiological terms, although within each of the sexes boys and girls undoubtedly vary greatly, across both sexes boys do appear to be the more sensitive, emotional sex.

There is a brain explanation for this difference in emotional sensitivity. As explained in Chapter 1, boys' brains have a larger amygdala (that "tiger" in their tanks; see page 18) that orchestrates all emotion. Coupled with this, recent research has revealed that another brain structure is also larger in males: this is the hormone releaser or hypothalamus. Together, these two structures operate to produce males' greater physical reactions in the face of emotion arousal.

Related to this research is the finding that boy babies tend to be more fractious than girls. Because they may be more demanding of their caregivers, mothers of sons may need to work harder than mothers of daughters to make their sons feel safe and secure. In the study that examined what happens when mothers returned to work before their sons were six months old (see page 141), although many of the boys were securely attached to their mothers, far fewer of them were securely attached to their *fathers* than boys or girls of non-employed mothers. This suggests that boys need longer than girls to build a strong, secure attachment with their mother and before they are ready to begin building strong attachments with others.

Boys' areas of vulnerability

○ Due to the different timetables of male and female brain development, early attachments may be more vulnerable and difficult to establish with boys than with girls. Because the regions in the front of the brain involved with social and emotional behavior develop earlier in girls than in boys (see page 70), little girls are inclined to be more social in their behavior and therefore tend to elicit more social responses from their parents than boys.

○ Boys have an innate desire to be top dog (due to their larger "tigers"). If they feel that their life is not a success in some way (parental divorce, failure at school), their badly dented pride may mean that even very secure attachments fail to provide them with adequate support.

○ A sex difference emerged when researchers investigated what contribution parents' hostility made to the development of behavior problems in children aged nine to thirteen. Parents who were hostile toward each other and hostile toward their child had more of an impact on boys' adjustment. In such circumstances, boys were more likely to be either abnormally withdrawn or physically aggressive.

○ Over 300 children in three age groups were observed at home interacting with their parents. At twelve and eighteen months of age, it was found that boys received more negative responses from both parents than girls did. Further, mothers gave less instruction to boys aged eighteen months than girls of this age when they tried to communicate.

○ Mothers of boys tail off in their verbal encouragements during the period when the babies are between four and eight months, but carry on throughout this period responding and communicating to their baby daughters just as much as they ever did (see page 46).

○ When over 1,500 children were monitored between the ages of five and eleven, more boys than girls displayed behavior that put them at risk, or met the criteria for conduct disorders in adolescence.

○ Other studies show links not only between boys' reading problems and bad behavior, but also between the nature of parent-son relationships and behavioral problems.

7 Mothers and sons

The mother-son relationship is the first relationship that a boy has with a member of the opposite sex. It will influence a boy's subsequent opposite-sex relationships more than any other. To complicate things, a mother is more likely to know instinctively how best to respond to a girl, not a boy. So, in times of stress or doubt, mothers may respond in a female way that may be fine for a girl, but is less appropriate for a boy.

As a result of such instinctive reactions, as a boy grows older, his mother's behavior toward him may strike him as being less consistent. He may feel that she responds positively only some of the time, intrusively and insensitively at other times. Moreover, although he once experienced an attachment with his mother of the secure variety, their relationship may drift more toward the anxious/ambivalent.

Mistakes mothers can make

All mothers are under a great deal of pressure and none is immune to making a few mistakes along the way. Three common mistakes are outlined here.

Mothers with hurt feelings

The most powerful way to ensure a child's bright outlook on life is to find ways to praise him and his behavior, redirecting misbehavior in positive ways that will preserve his self-esteem. However, one of the female strategies mothers may fall back on in times of stress is to focus on feelings – *their* feelings. Whereas girls, with their earlier frontal lobe development, may be more capable of empathizing with their mothers, boys subjected to this strategy may not fare so well. A boy, with the more urgent need to preserve his ego, understands only that his mother's love is suddenly a lot less predictable than before. For him, it is a maternal strategy that operates only to erode his self-esteem and sense of security.

It may come in the shape of an outburst at the supermarket: "Stop that at once! How can you embarrass me like this in front of all these people!" Or, on other occasions: "Philip! How can you be so cruel? You don't really want to go on the school trip, when you can stay at home and have a nice time with me and your family?" or, "Stephen, if you do that, you will

really hurt my feelings." These are the sort of remarks and veiled threats that make a boy feel enormously guilty, that can add up to convince him that he is a thoughtless, selfish, heartless human being.

Mothers over-eager to help

Whereas a girl is inclined to feel loved and validated when others offer to help or advise, a boy's ego receives a much bigger boost if he is allowed to do something on his own. Mothers, in particular, may underestimate a boy's need to be trusted as a capable decision-maker and performer. Studies reveal that boys receive far more direction and advice from their mothers than from their fathers. A mother's tendency to offer unsolicited advice when her son misbehaves, makes mistakes or appears to need help is what psychologists call "Mrs. Home Improvement" behavior.

A female's desire to improve things around the home often extends, once she is a mother, to her children. Unlike a girl, a boy feels *less* cared for if his mother tries to "improve" him. He wants her to find him acceptable and competent just the way he is! He views masses of instruction and advice from his mother as a criticism of who he is.

Mothers who betray their son's trust

Without really being aware of it, a mother may betray her son's trust. This can happen simply with a few thoughtless comments (see box above). A girl may more easily forgive her mother's social insensitivity. In a boy's case, if the wound inflicted is deep enough, he may grow up to be a man who finds it difficult to trust a woman with his feelings.

More seriously, some mothers may inadvertently cause their sons to grow up with a deep-seated fear of, or anger toward, women they care about. This can happen when a mother (on whom her son is wholly emotionally dependent) routinely betrays him, for example, by reporting on his misdeeds to an aloof father who dishes out harsh physical punishment (more common if the child is a boy).

In such circumstances, boys can grow up to be incapable of healthy relationships with members of the opposite sex. They are likely to have highly controlling personalities, often emotionally and/or physically abusive toward their partners – the angry tyrants of this world. For such a man, the thought of a woman having control over him (via his emotional dependency upon her) is terrifying to contemplate.

7 Fathers and sons

Although boys' initial attachment is usually to their mothers, by the second year of life, most boys develop a secure attachment to their fathers as well. Indeed, in one study, it was found that during the second year of life, although girls did not display any consistent preferences, boys began to demonstrate more interest and interaction with their fathers. In fact, by the end of the second year, all but one boy in the sample seemed to have a stronger paternal than maternal attachment.

Fathers should not wait until their son is eight or ten years old before they become more involved in his life. In one study, infants' intellectual and motor development scores were higher if the father had been actively involved during the first six months of the child's life. Furthermore, in another study, children were found to manage stress better during their school years if their fathers had been intimately involved during the first *eight weeks* of their infancy.

New research is revealing that children benefit from close relationships with both their parents *throughout* infancy, childhood and into adolescence.

On a separate issue, there is some controversy. Are mothers or fathers needed more by their sons and daughters at certain stages of their lives? A popular view is that a boy's relationship with his mother undergoes a transformation around the age of ten and that his father becomes a much more important figure in his life. Although there does not seem to be any evidence to support this, there is a modest amount of evidence to suggest that, after the age of fourteen, some boys may spend more time engaged in activities with, and seek the advice of, their fathers (and some girls may turn more to their mothers).

I felt like running away

Fathers can tell their sons about certain moments in their own lives to demonstrate that it's OK for a male to make mistakes or reveal weakness. For example, a father could describe the time he tried out for the football team and how terrified he was that he would make a fool of himself. Then he can ask his son if he has ever felt that way.

Boys need mothers *and* fathers

Both mothers and fathers make mistakes. Research shows that serious personality-related problems of parents (alcoholism, violence, depression, criminality) can cause similar maladjustment problems in children. Perhaps this is part of the reason why studies also show that children generally fare better in two-parent than single-parent families.

Since mothers and fathers parent children differently, perhaps two-parent children enjoy a more balanced experience overall. Studies do show that children from two-parent families tend to perform better than their single-parent peers both academically and emotionally.

This does not mean, however, that single parents cannot bring up successful, well-adjusted children. Many of the studies undertaken in this area fail to take into account the effects of social class and poverty, factors than can account for a large portion of the negative effects of single-parent families.

Successful single parents

Take heart! Many single parents are succeeding brilliantly with their children. Research shows that successful single parents have

○ greater available financial resources, enhancing their coping effectiveness;

○ better family organization to balance household responsibilities and decrease task overload;

○ a positive family concept: valuing loyalty, home, consideration, communication and closeness;

○ an ability to highlight the positive and downplay the negative aspects of a stressful event;

○ supportive, stress-reducing social networks.

7 Working together

Ask any parent what they most want for their child and the answer is almost always "happiness." Most parents recognize that the happiest children are the ones with a strong sense of self-worth and whose needs are understood, responded to and respected. In spite of their growing independence, these are the children whose parents are able to maintain a close bond with them throughout their childhood and adolescence. Most parents do their utmost to ensure that their children experience exactly this. However, like the rest of the human race, parents are not infallible.

Parenting is not a straightforward life choice. Babies and teenagers have different requirements. Researchers have observed that in times of stress or doubt, parents may be forced to switch to "automatic-pilot" mode. At such times, they may unthinkingly resort to stereotypical parenting behavior – behavior that may well reflect that of their parents or grandparents, that they would not normally display. Such reactions in times of uncertainty can have different effects on boys and girls.

Complementary parenting

Although some research suggests that adolescent girls spend greater amounts of time with their mothers than their fathers, and vice versa for boys, this is something that appears to happen more often in families that adhere to stereotypical gender roles. In general, research supports the idea that boys who have close connections at all ages with both their parents benefit the most.

Because mothers and fathers differ in their parenting styles, children exposed to these different styles learn more. A boy, whether he is younger or older, who is securely attached to both parents can more fully develop his own sexual identity and better relate to people of both sexes in the outside world.

Some parenting tasks may be more difficult for fathers to accomplish, some for mothers. When mothers and fathers cooperate and love each other, their different ways of parenting will provide a balanced set of experiences for their son. While avoiding a situation where the child plays one parent off against the other, of course, mothers and fathers can provide complementary ways of approaching the many different aspects of parenting.

Interacting

The physical rough-and-tumble play that fathers engage in gives boys practice in regulating their emotions and behavior. Mothers, who cuddle their babies more, make their sons feel safe. The two styles of interacting communicate love and physical intimacy and, together, they operate to increase a boy's confidence and sense of security.

Challenging

Fathers encourage their sons to take chances and push themselves harder, whereas mothers issue more cautions. Whereas one style encourages risk without considering consequences, the other avoids risk and may fail to build independence, confidence and progress. One style complements the other.

Communicating

Mothers' and fathers' different styles of communicating help boys learn how to converse with their own and the opposite sex.

Disciplining

One parent may be the one who tends to enforce rules, systematically teaching the consequences of right and wrong, whereas the other may tend toward sympathy and leniency. Boys need high levels of both control and nurturing. The first, on its own, leads to anxiety and insecurity. The second, on its own, leads to a lack of self-discipline. Together, the two styles provide a healthy balance.

Loosening the reins

A tricky part of parenting is to recognize that the best way to maintain close emotional ties as your son grows older is to show that you trust him and respect his growing desire to be independent by

loosening the reins. This latter task may be more difficult for mothers than fathers. A mother's style of parenting tends to focus on nurturing and protecting and a father's on preparing and challenging. So letting go (even if it *is* the best route to *preserving* close emotional ties) is inclined to feel unnatural to mothers.

Protecting

Fathers help their children prepare for the realities and harshness of the world, whereas mothers want to help their children avoid dangerous or unpleasant experiences in their lives. Both influences are necessary as a boy grows into adulthood.

Being

Mothers give their sons an insight into the female world, helping them understand how to relate to women. Fathers help their sons understand male sexuality and behavior, how to channel their frustrations and anger in positive ways and how to overcome their fear of being labeled "a girl" when revealing their vulnerabilities.

Interacting with the opposite sex

Boys learn how to respect and interact with women by observing their parents' relationship. They can emulate their successes and learn from their failures.

7 Teenage brain growth and the big T

During adolescence, there are three main influences that affect boys' behavior and personality development.

- There is a new burst of development in the higher, frontal region of the brain.
- Testosterone levels rise to their highest peak.
- Peers become a much more important part of a boy's life.

New brain growth

Less than ten years ago scientists thought that the brain stopped growing during early childhood. Then, much to everyone's surprise, it was discovered that, prior to puberty, there is a second burst of new growth in the upper frontal region of the brain, a region directly involved in social behavior, mood and impulse control. So a number of the personality characteristics associated with teenage boys are caused not by hormones, but by brain changes.

Not only is this late phase of brain development later in boys than girls, but because of their larger amygdalas ("tigers") urging emotional responses, a teenage boy cannot handle social pressure, instinctual urges and other stresses as well as a girl of the same age. Your son may listen to you and agree with your arguments against, say, drugs and alcohol, but when he's with his friends, he acts purely on impulse. His amygdala takes over. His brain is simply not yet mature, and it may take some time. Researchers at the University of McMaster in Ontario, Canada, found that after male university students viewed pictures of pretty women their ability to think about consequences became impaired.

The new wave of brain growth in the frontal region is followed by an extended period during which the synaptic connections and

neural networks are pruned and refined. Environmental experience at this time (from the age of twelve to the late twenties) is critical in shaping how the brain wires itself up. Only recently, research revealed that alcohol and nicotine, for example, cause far more damaging effects to the teenage than the adult brain. Boys appear to be more vulnerable than girls to these and other environmental influences because their development begins later and is slower. Indeed, separate research indicates that adolescent boys are more suggestible than adolescent girls.

The big T: it's testosterone time again!

Delinquency, violence, recklessness, mood swings or irresponsible behavior: testosterone is to blame. At least, this often seems to be the standard view. Is there any truth in it? From nine to thirteen, boys' testosterone levels increase as much as five times; in fact, overall (from the age of nine to twenty) they can increase as much as nineteen times. Surely this unprecedented influx of hormones is bound to have some effect on a boy's personality development.

The testosterone that floods an adolescent's body does produce some major physical changes that can also affect personality development. Acne, lack of facial hair, inappropriate voice changes and worry over penis size can all undermine a young boy's self-confidence. An increased sex drive and interest in sex can lead to fear of exposure, tiredness, irritability and lack of concentration.

Apart from the well-documented pubertal changes and the related personality side effects, the research linking testosterone with behavior is plagued with inconsistency. While some studies suggest that high testosterone levels increase violence and aggression, more often it seems that aggression can cause testosterone levels to rise. However, once levels have risen, they can add "fuel to the fire" and enhance aggression. To add to the complexity of this picture, testosterone levels can vary by as much as 50 percent

in the same day, and peaks do not necessarily coincide with when a male is at his most aggressive.

Since a number of different hormones act in the body in tandem, it is inaccurate to attribute specific personality characteristics to a single hormone. It seems likely that a truer picture is that certain environmental factors or situations act in concert with hormonal influences to provoke particular behavior.

Social circumstances, such as quality of parental relationship, social rank among peers, the degree of sexual arousal or level of competition or conflict, can all influence testosterone levels.

○ In boys aged six to eighteen, as parent-child relationship quality increases, testosterone-related adjustment problems become less evident.

○ Thirteen-year-old boys with a history of unpopularity among their peers, failure at school and physical aggressiveness are found to have low testosterone levels. Boys rated as socially dominant and popular are found to have high levels of testosterone.

○ Testosterone levels surge dramatically, by as much as 30 percent, when males meet and try to impress an attractive female.

○ Prior to and during physical (or non-physical) competition, males' testosterone levels rise. After a game of football, for example, the winners' testosterone levels have been found to remain high, while the losers' levels decline. This pattern occurs among the fans as well.

Biological factors also influence testosterone levels: amounts of stress hormones circulating in the bloodstream, base levels of testosterone and the degree to which there is a predisposition toward aggression. To illustrate this, when testosterone injections are given, the reported effects are extremely wide-ranging: from an increase in self-confidence, well-being, euphoria, drive, swagger and the ability to "take charge" to irritability and a tendency to frustration and edginess.

7 The inestimable influence of peer pressure

Although friendships are important to both boys and girls during childhood, there is a major change for both sexes during adolescence. As they struggle to develop their own identities, a dependence upon parents gives way to a new dependence upon their peers. Try to convince your son that it doesn't matter if he hasn't got a tattoo like his friend or isn't allowed to go to a particular rock concert, and you won't succeed, for the simple reason that it *does* matter to him. A lot.

For girls, conforming with their peers matters because they need to feel accepted by and emotionally connected to them, but for boys, it is more about competition, the need to maintain or jostle for a higher social rank among their peers.

Although for both boys and girls, relationships with peers become more intimate during adolescence, their different needs result in different ways of bringing this about. Girls establish intimacy through discussion and self-disclosure, whereas boys grow closer to their friends through shared activities. To accomplish these goals, girls more often get together in pairs whereas boys are more likely to spend time together in larger groups.

Research on peer relationships during adolescence highlights the following gender differences:

○ For boys, the ideal male is "hard" (that is, tall, muscular, assertive), good at sports, attractive to girls and not "girlish." He has established emotional distance from his mother, has increased intimacy with his father and is not too studious. For girls, high on the list are social popularity, physical attractiveness and academic capability.

○ Relationships with friends play a significant role in whether teenage girls think about suicide, but have little impact on suicidal thoughts among boys.

○ Boys more often use physical aggression to establish social order and respond to it more than girls.

Girls use verbal aggression more often than physical means to manipulate social relationships; girls are more "hurt" by this strategy.

○ While evidence shows that all adolescents worry about opposite sex romantic relationships more than any other issue, boys tend to worry less and place less importance on them than girls do.

Fitting in with the crowd

In early adolescence, boys begin to challenge parental authority, rules and values, and compare pubertal changes with their same-sex peers. They worry about being different from their friends and go to great lengths to look and behave like other boys.

As they grow older, teenage boys spend more time with their peers and away from their families. The development of their sense of self is the focus, as they reassess, accept, reject or modify society's norms. They must make up their own minds about who they are and what they believe in. Maintaining their social position may become increasingly demanding socially and academically. The ability to attract girls increases status, whereas revealing responsible and studious tendencies can diminish it.

One large U.S. study followed students over four years, from thirteen to seventeen years of age. It found the influence of adolescent peers explained student behavior throughout that time better than any variable.

The teenage boy: what can you do to help?

○ Take care not to embarrass your son in front of his friends by talking about homework, for example, or how he did on a test. He will be more inclined to apply himself academically if he knows he can count on you not to destroy his credibility with friends.

○ Avoid dismissing or criticizing his friends. These are the people who are most important to his self-concept right now. They provide him with a sense of status and belonging.

○ You cannot eliminate peer pressure but you can dilute it by providing a balancing influence. Help him choose a school where boys are performing as well as girls academically. Instead of telling him he must work hard so that he can go to college, make it clear that education gives him the luxury of choice.

○ Becoming sexually active is an important step in every person's life. Keeping open the lines of communication with your teenager is most important to ensure that he is knowledgeable about the consequences of engaging in unsafe behavior. Show that you trust your son to behave responsibly. This gives him an incentive to live up to your expectations. Constant prying or suspicion has the opposite effect.

Having academically oriented friends seemed to encourage students to behave well and helped them resist drugs and alcohol, whereas, a negative peer influence seemed to greatly increase a student's risk for behavioral problems and substance abuse.

7 Parents can bring out the best in boys

Although peers do play a prominent role during adolescence, parents are central to shaping their son's personality. Society today, however, places high expectations on both mothers and fathers. Mothers are now expected not only to hold down a career but also to find time to do the bulk of the housework and child care. Studies reveal that in two-career marriages, mothers still do more than 60–70 percent of the housework and child care.

Traditionally, fathers were expected to support their families. But now, they are expected to make a much larger contribution than in the past to the day-to-day child care and housework as well. In the past, a male's sights were singularly focused on being a good provider for his family, but now fathers are made to feel guilty for spending too much time focused on their careers. In a 2001 government survey of over 1,200 British men, more than two-thirds said that despite working long hours, they were spending more time with their children than their fathers had done. But revealing a general sense of guilt, almost half said that their work prevented them from spending as much time with their children as they would like.

There is a limit to what one person can accomplish and, for single parents (especially women), bringing up a boy may seem a particularly challenging responsibility. However, as long as you simply do the best you can to keep your son emotionally close, there is no need to worry or to feel guilty. The research is convincing. Boys who are close to their parents (or to a parent) generally have brains that grow faster, have a large circle of friends, do well at school, stay out of trouble and are happier and more successful.

Helping your son through his growing years

Here are some final tips on how to enhance the quality of parent-son relationships.

- The closer the emotional ties between you and your son, the healthier, happier and more intelligent he is likely to be.

- Respond to your baby son's cries. The more you do, the less he will cry.

- Maximize physical contact with your son – cuddle him, carry him close to you, massage him.

- Follow your son's cues to determine his sleeping schedules when he's an infant.

- Read to your son and/or listen to him read daily.

- Use positive discipline, not punitive discipline or corporal punishment.

- Co-parent; share the development of secure parent-child attachments with your partner.

- Set clear expectations and guidelines for your son's behavior, as well as consequences for breaking them. Saying "no" to your son's more unreasonable demands is very important to his future happiness.

- Give your son plenty of love and affection. Boys can misinterpret, so don't forget to provide verbal reassurances that you love him as well.

- Monitor his development in an interested, non-controlling way. Get to know his friends, his teachers, what he watches on television and what music he listens to.

- Talk to him frequently about his interests, hopes, fears and desires.

- Model equity between sexes. Both parents should share in family responsibilities at home and outside the home if possible.

- From an early age, give your son developmentally appropriate responsibilities and chores.

- Share specific hobbies or activities with your son, but don't forget to talk to him at the same time.

- If possible, involve your son in activities that have status among his peers, or that will teach him skills that will be useful when he's older – team games, martial arts, guitar, singing, windsurfing, skiing, sailing, cycling, fishing, dancing, tennis, golf.

- If divorced, try to minimize conflict with your "ex."

- Include your son in the creation and enforcement of house rules.

- Give him age-appropriate freedoms, showing that you trust him.

- Listen to and respect his views, encouraging him to think for himself.

- Finally, have fun together. The key to your son's resilience is his sense of self-esteem. He will be happiest if you love him for who he is, not what you'd like him to be or what he might achieve.

index

further reading

Ainsworth, M., Blehar, M. Waters, E., & Wall, S. (1978). *Patterns of attachment.* Hillsdale, NJ: Erlbaum.

ARUP (2004). *ARUP's guide to clinical laboratory testing: Testosterone.* University of Utah Associated Regional and University Pathology of ARUP Laboratories.

Allen, L.S., Richey, M.F., Chai, Y.M., Gorski, R.A. (1991). Sex differences in the corpus callosum of the living human being. *Journal of Neuroscience, 11(4),* 933-42.

Baron-Cohen, S. (2003). Sugar and spice. (Link between fetal testosterone levels and vocabulary at 18 months). *New Scientist, 12th May,* pp. 54-55.

Cahan, S. & Cohan, N. (1989). Age versus schooling effects on intelligence development. *Child Development, 60,* 1239-49.

Ceci, S. J. (1991). How much does schooling influence general intelligence and its cognitive components? A reassessment of the evidence. *Developmental Psychology, 27,* 703-22.

Clark, D.L., Kreutzberg, J.R., & Chee, F.K. (1977). Vestibular stimulation influence on motor development in infants. *Science, 196,* 1228-29.

Eliot, L. (1999). *Early intelligence.* London: Penguin Books.

Fenson, L., Dale, P.S., Reznick, J.S., Bates, E., Thal, D.J., Pethick. S.J. (1994). Variability in early communicative development. *Monographs in Social Research and Child Development, 59* (5), 1-173.

Forget, H. & Cohen, H. (1994). Life after birth: the influence of steroid hormones on cerebral structure and function is not fixed prenatally. *Brain and Cognition, 26,* 243-248.

Fowler, W. (1990). *Talking from infancy: How to nurture and cultivate early language development*. Cambridge, MA: Brookline Books.

Frederikse, M. F., Lu, A., Aylward, E., Barta, P., Pearlson, G. (1999). Sex differences in the inferior parietal lobule. *Cerebral Cortex, 9* (8), 896-901.

Fryberg, E. (1997). *Reading and learning disabilities: a neuropsychological approach to evaluation and instruction*. Springfield, Illinois: Charles C Thomas Publisher.

Goleman, D. (1997). Emotional intelligence: why it can matter more than IQ. (Describes Walter Mischel's 'marshmallow test' experiment). NY: Bantam Books.

Giedd, J.N., Castellanons, F.X., Rajapakse, J.C., Vaituzis, A.C., Rappapport, J.L. (1996). Sexual dipmorphism of the developing human brain. *Progress in Neuro-psychopharmacology, Biology and Psychiatry, 21* (8), 1185-201.

Gur, R.C., Gunning-Dixon, F., Bilker, W.B., Gur, R.E. (2002). Sex differences in temporo-limbic and frontal brain volumes of healthy adults. *Cerebral Cortex, 12* (9), 998-1003.

Halpern, D. F. (1992). *Sex differences in cognitive abilities*. Hillsdale, NJ: Lawrence Erlbaum.

Hanlon, H. W., Thatcher, R. W., Cline, M. J. (1999). Gender differences in the development of EEG coherence in normal children. *Developmental Neuropsychology, 16* (3), 479-506.

Hart, B. & Risley, T.R. (1995). *Meaningful differences in the everday experience of young American children*. Baltimore: Paul H. Brooks.

Hyde, J.S., Fennema, E., Lamon, S.J. (1990). Gender differences in mathematics performance: a meta-analysis. *Psychological Bulletin, 107* (2), 139-55.

Johnston, R.S. & Watson, J.E. (2003). Accelerating the development of reading, spelling and phonemic awareness skills in initial readers. *Reading and Writing: An Interdisciplinary Journal, 00*, 1-31. (pre-publication online: http://www.kluweronline.com/issn/0922-4777/contents)

Karass, J., Julia, M., Braungart-Rieker, J.M., Mullins, J., Lefever, J.B. (2002). Process in language acquisition: the roles of gender, attention, and maternal encouragement of attention over time. *Journal of Child Language, 29*, 519-543.

Kimura, D. (1999). *Sex and Cognition*. Cambridge, MS: MIT Press.

Kramer, J.H., Ellenberg, L., Leonard J., Share, L.J. (1996). Developmental sex differences in global-local perceptual bias. *Neuropsychology, 10* (3), 402-07.

Leake, J. (2003). A taste of fish puts failing pupils on top. September 28th, News section, *The Sunday Times*, p. 6.

Levine, S., Huttenlocher, J., Taylor, A., & Lansgrock, A. (1999). Early sex differences in spatial skill. *Developmental Psychology, 35* (4), 940-9.

Lucas, A., Morley, R., Cole, T.J., Lister, G., Leeson-Payne, C. (1992). Breast milk and subsequent intelligence quotient in children born pre-term. *Lancet, 339*, 261-64.

Macmillan, B. (2002). An evaluation of the government's early intervention initiative: The Early Literacy Support Programme. *Reading Reform Foundation, Newsletter No. 49*, Autumn, 11-15.

Macmillan, B.J. (1997). *Why schoolchildren can't read*. London: Institute of Economic Affairs.

McLaughlin, L. & Park, A. (2000). The testosterone effect, *Time Europe, 155* (16), April 24.

Nicolson, R., Fawcett, A.J., Berry, E.L., Jenkins, H., Dean, P., Brooks, D.J. (1998). Association of abnormal cerebellar activation with motor learning difficulties in dyslexic adults. *Lancet, 353*, 1662-67.

Philips, S., Steele, S., Tanz, C. (Eds.) (1987). *Language, Gender and Sex in Comparative Perspective*. NY: Cambridge University Press.

PIRLS: Mullis, I., Martin, M., Gonzalez, E., Kennedy, A. (2003). *PIRLS international report: IEA's study of reading literacy achievement in primary schools*. Chestnut Hill, MA: Boston College.

PISA: Organization for Economic Co-operation and Development, UNESCO Institute for Statistics (2003). *Literacy skills for the world of tomorrow – Further results from PISA 2000*. Paris, France: OECD Publications.

Simos, P.G., Fletcher, J.M., Bergman, E., Breier, J.I., Foorman, B.R., Castillo, E.M., Davis, R.N., Fitzgerald, M., Panpanicolaou, A.C. (2002). Dyslexia-specific brain activation profile become normal following successful remedial training. *Neurology, 58* (8), 1203-13.

Shucard, J.L. & Shucard, D.W. (1990). Auditory evoked potentials and hand preference in 6-month-old infants: possible gender-related differences in cerebral organization. *Developmental Psychology, 26* (6), 923-930.

Soderman, A., Chhikara, S., Chen Hsiu-Ching, & Kuo, E. (1999). Gender differences that affect emergent literacy in first grade children: USA, India and Taiwan. *International Journal of Early Childhood, 31* (2), 9-16.

Waters, E., Crowell, J., Elliot, M., Corcoran, D., & Treboux, D. (2002). *Attachment and Human Development*, 4, 230-42.

Weizman, Z. & Snow, C.E. (2001). Lexical input as related to children's vocabulary acquisition: effects of sophisticated exposure and support for meaning. *Developmental Psychology, 37*, 265-279.

acknowledgments

Author acknowledgments

I would like to thank my editors, Jessica Cowie, Caroline Ball, and Nikki Sims
for their useful, insightful comments and suggestions. Their patience and efficiency
has been much appreciated. I am particularly grateful to Jane McIntosh who initially conceived
the idea for this book and who has been unfailing in her
kind support throughout the project.

Publisher acknowledgments

Executive Editor **Jane McIntosh**
Project Editor **Jessica Cowie**
Executive Art Editor **Jo MacGregor**
Designer **Ruth Hope**
Illustration **Cactus Design and Illustration Ltd**
Picture Research **Luzia Strohmayer/Aruna Mathur**
Assistant Production Controller **Aileen O'Reilly**

Picture credits

Special Photography by Adrian Pope

Corbis UK Ltd 23, 150, 152/Owen Franken 111/Roy Morsch 82 bottom left
Getty Images 1, 14, 30 top center, 36 top, 85, 90 left, 90 center, 93, 98, 134 center, 149
Octopus Publishing Group Limited/David Jordan 84/Sandra Lousada 38/Leo Mason 105/Mark Newcombe
106/Peter Pugh-Cook 2, 6, 8 top centre, 8 top left, 8 top right, 10, 11, 15, 16 top right, 16 bottom left, 17, 18,
20, 21 bottom right, 30 top left, 32, 33, 34 top, 34 bottom, 36 bottom, 39 top right, 39 bottom left, 40 top right,
40 bottom left, 41, 42, 43, 47, 48 top, 54, 55 bottom left, 57, 58, 59, 60, 61, 62, 62 top left, 63 top right, 63 top
center right, 63 top center left, 66, 69 bottom, 72, 73, 74 left, 74 right, 77, 79, 80 top, 80 bottom, 82, 92, 94, 95,
96, 97, 100, 101 bottom right, 103, 108 left, 108 right, 108 center, 112, 116, 118, 120, 122, 123, 124 left, 128
top, 129, 130, 132, 134 right, 138, 139, 140, 141, 142, 143, 144, 147/Gareth Sambidge 35